BETTY CROCKER'S
Growing Your Own Houseplants

By Jacqueline Hériteau

GOLDEN PRESS • NEW YORK
Western Publishing Company, Inc.
Racine, Wisconsin

Four-color photographs by George
Ancona, with the following exceptions:
page 9, John Garetti; page 37, courtesy
Ball Seed Company; pages 47, 49 and 54,
Malak Photographs Limited; page 50,
Pedro E. Guerrero.
Black-and-white photographs
by John Garetti.
Illustrations by Frank Fretz.

Printed in the U.S.A. Published by
Golden Press, New York, N.Y.
Library of Congress Catalog Card
Number: 76-52635
*Betty Crocker is a registered trademark
of General Mills, Inc.
Golden and Golden Press® are registered
trademarks of Western Publishing
Company, Inc.

CONTENTS

HOUSEPLANTS FROM SCRATCH

You are about to embark on what may be the most fascinating trip you will ever take—a trip through the very essence of nature.

When you buy mature, flourishing plants from greenhouses or from florists, you buy beauty and elegance. But when you start your own plants from scratch or dig them up in the wild, you learn how things really are on our small planet, and see a will to survive that seems absolutely exotic in its manifestations. Plants can do things that people can't do.

Imagine what it would be like if, from a limb, you could grow a brand-new person! And if the body were to replace that limb by growing a brand-new part! Wild, right? There could be dozens of you, depending on how many limbs you were willing to lop off and root. Well, when it comes to making dozens of plants where a single one grew before, it's not at all "wild"—it's what growers do. They remove a leaf or a branch tip, and each develops into a whole new plant, from the root up to the last flowering detail, a perfect double of the parent, without harming the parent. The parent just grows new leaves or tips to replace the borrowed ones.

To the indoor gardener who wants free plants by the dozen, dividing to multiply is one of the best ways to go. Reproduction of plant parts, however, is only one of the many ways by which you can acquire indoor greenery without spending money.

Most plants are propagated from seeds, and free seeds are available from your own or friends' houseplants, from citrus fruits—even from your spice shelf. It costs nothing to experiment, and the results may be priceless. On the other hand, though you can grow geraniums and wax begonias from seeds, a faster way to get mature plants is to root cut ends of branches.

In the vegetable kingdom, seeds are a relatively modern means of reproduction. Ferns, among the oldest vegetation known on the planet, develop no seeds. Instead they spread spores bearing a dust-like reproductive substance; with patience you can develop a houseful of ferns by spore propagation.

You can depend upon, and borrow from, nature's unthwartable will to survive individually in all its creations. The list of nature's ways and means is probably endless. You can grow a tiny forest of ferny leaves from a cut-up carrot, and a beautiful pineapple plant from pineapple leaves. Carrots and pineapples are programmed to spread their kind, and the key to their propagation is in the foliage; cut-off tops grow new foliage.

Other plants, those not gifted with the ability to reproduce from torn leaves and limbs, can reproduce whole new plants from small root divisions. The spider plant grows graceful nests of leaves at the tips of slender, cascading stems. Give them soil, and they will root and form new plants. Ivy creeps along the ground or down the sides of its containers in search not only of light for new leaves but for new ground to root in. Supply it, and you'll have dozens of ivy plants.

Nature has further guaranteed survival by making plants ever so adaptive. Plants that love sun and open skies are so willing to follow their growth instinct that they'll adapt to indoor sill light and the artificial light of fluorescent bulbs. Wild woodland plants will pretend that a terrarium or a bottle garden is home. Big plants from the outdoors, set in small containers, will become small plants for the indoors; and it is on this dwarfing principle that the art of bonsai is based. Plants that grow naturally as shrubs become trees if pruned in tree shapes. Flowering branches and spring bulbs will bloom indoors in late winter as though it were the cool, moist outdoors of spring. You can use all these adaptive faculties to fill your home with almost every type of plant imaginable.

In taming your new wildlings, nurtured seedlings and fresh cuttings, and in bringing all your treasures of green to flourishing maturity, you will find that you are growing plants better adapted to the conditions in your house than the greenhouse specimens you buy and bring home. In the process of acquiring, rather than buying, plants, you will learn to care for them, to be so sensitive to their needs that from a half-conscious glance you'll read barely visible signals—"water needed," "food wanted"—so quickly that you would say it is intuition, not knowledge, speaking.

And that's how great indoor gardens come into being—through the sensitive, loving care of a novice who grows in knowledge while the plants he or she creates grow in maturity.

Woodland ferns make a striking permanent display. Choose containers to complement room decor; add seasonal accents for variety.

OUTDOOR PLANTS: YOURS FOR THE DIGGING

If you want to turn your home into a greenhouse overnight, look outdoors. It's winter? Turn to page 26 and you'll see that the outdoors has gifts for you even at this season of the year when all seems lifeless. In early fall, you will find supplies for indoor growing in your flower garden and in containers and window boxes. In spring, you'll find a new crop of houseplants among the wild plants coming to life in the woods and by the roadside.

Plants from the Garden

When the first frosts of fall are on their way, do you wistfully say goodbye to your brilliantly blooming marigolds, brave pink petunias and flourishing window-box ivies and just let them die of cold? With marigolds, it is a little less sad: These are annuals that finish their life cycle at the end of the season, so their passing is hastened, not caused, by the cold. But geraniums are perennials and live on and on in warm climates. So are the tender ivies and many other container and garden plants you let go each fall.

Plants commonly grown outdoors that can be brought in include balsam, begonia, coleus, geranium, impatiens, lantana, lobelia, petunia, marigold, fuchsia, browallia, caladium, the tender English ivies, myrtle, alpine straw-

berry and many herbs as well. This list does not include *all* the outdoor plants that can be brought in. It does include popular plants grown across the country that will fade in the fall and probably die if they spend the winter outdoors.

Many varieties of English ivy and myrtle are hardy (withstand cold), and so are alpine strawberries. However, since some of the most attractive varieties won't stand the cold, and even some hardy types may die in window boxes and containers, these, too, are considered good subjects to bring in.

Bringing In Flowering Plants

The lovely summer flowering plants, covered with bright blossoms, will make a glorious show when brought in the fall. Many will live only for awhile after they come in; other plants may live all winter indoors.

Since some of these plants make fine homes for white flies, select the ones you plan to bring in carefully and clean daily with a fine spray of water for several weeks before you move them. The first few days indoors, spray them in the kitchen sink to discourage any remaining pests.

A few weeks before the move, pot up the plants and cut back the end third of each branch. Feed the plants weekly before the move and after you bring them indoors. Keep the soil evenly moist and mist daily. Place the plants in light similar to what they received when outdoors. When they begin to fade, try rooting tip cuttings (see page 58) to provide new plants to set out next spring, and discard the parent plants. Lantana and browallia may succeed indoors all winter if kept in a cool, sunny spot. If they fade, rest them in a cool (40 to 50 degrees), dark

spot. Keep almost dry until spring. Then cut back the branch ends by half, repot in fresh potting soil, feed a blooming-type plant food weekly and set outdoors when the weather warms.

Marigolds in full bloom can fill a room with sunshine. I have brought in the giant Climax marigolds and French and dwarf marigolds. They last about six weeks, but eventually succumb to white flies or red spider-mites—so keep them isolated from other houseplants. Follow the instructions above for bringing them in, but do not cut away any branch ends. The big Climax plants are the size of bushes by summer's end, and you have to really want them to go to the trouble of transplanting them. The small marigolds are easy to plant in big ceramic pots filled with soil from the garden. Keep moist. When the leaves begin to brown, discard the plants.

Geraniums will last all winter and in a sunny window will keep blooming. The easiest geraniums to bring in are those that were set out in their greenhouse pots. Plants rooted in the ground must have roots trimmed by about a third before they are brought in. Plant in all-purpose soil with one additional part sand or perlite. Don't trim branch ends or you'll cut away the blooms to come. Set in full sun and water when dry. Toward midwinter they'll get leggy. Cut back to compact size, and root tip ends so you'll have fresh geraniums to set out in spring. Handle ivy-leaf geraniums the same way, but cut all the branches back by a third in January. Poke the cut ends back into the pot or hanging basket to root. Keep all geraniums in a cool room.

The brightly flowered little wax begonias, which often are used to edge gardens, do very well indoors.

Dig them up, trim back the roots and tops by a third, pot in African-violet soil and place in a sunny east or west window at temperatures between 60 and 70 degrees. Keep the planting evenly moist, never soggy wet. If the tops get leggy, cut them back and root some tip cuttings to transplant in next year's garden.

The recently popular 'Rieger begonias,' which are tuberous rooted, make a glorious display all winter in cool temperatures if they have sun from an east, west or south window.

Bringing In Foliage Plants
Coleus is a foliage plant that grows very large outdoors. You can dig

up whole plants in fall, but a better way to fill the house with colorful coleus branches is to cut branch ends back to the ground before the cold weather arrives to wither them. Root these cuttings in big vases of water. Keep flowering tips pinched back to keep the plants compact. Transplant rooted branches together to make a nice

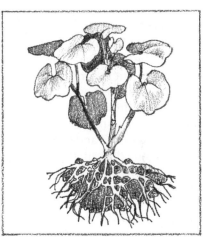

Trim geranium roots, but blooms will be lost if foliage is trimmed.

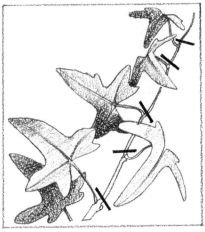

Trim marks at nodes on ivy branch show correct location for pruning all plants.

Left: When garden plants are brought in, they should be trimmed back by a third. Note trim marks on impatiens.

display. Plant in all-purpose soil and set in a sunny east, west or south window—the more sun, the more colorful the leaves. Keep the soil evenly moist and feed all-purpose plant food every two to four weeks. In spring, root new cuttings.

Caladiums grown in containers may be brought indoors in areas where they are not winter hardy. However, they soon go into a dormant stage. Remove them to a cool spot (40 to 50 degrees) and keep on the dry side until it is time to set them out in spring.

Alpine strawberries last indoors only in cool, fresh, moist air—with sun. Pot several in one large bulb pan in garden soil and keep evenly moist. If they dry out, they wither. Grow in direct sun.

English ivies, especially the small-leaved types and bird's-foot varieties, make durable and easy houseplants once they take hold. Dig up your plants, trim branch tips and roots back a third and pot in all-purpose soil. Feed all-purpose plant food monthly, provide fresh air often and mist daily. These are low-light plants that succeed in north windows, or east and west windows a few feet back from the direct sun.

Myrtle grows well indoors if kept cool and misted often. Follow the procedure for ivy (above), but plant in African-violet soil.

Keeping Your Houseplants Happy

When you bring outdoor plants in, you are drastically changing their environment. On pages 6–7 and above there are suggestions for care that will keep them in good condition for as long as possible. But an overview of the help they all need when they change homes will be good to keep in mind.

The key words are "change of environment." Plants that grow all year 'round indoors are acclimatized. Your new arrivals are not. Fresh air is vital to them, more fresh air than you probably give your houseplants (which need it, too). Open doors or windows during the warm part of the day and really air out rooms where your plants are growing. This will also bring temperatures down, and that's good, since most homes are overheated from a plant's point of view (unless it's a tropical plant). Freshening the air brings in moisture as well.

When the weather gets so cold that you can air only a few minutes a day without wrecking the heating budget, keep the air moist around your plants by misting them daily—even more often if you have the time. Misting helps plants survive temperatures that are really too warm for them, and so it is especially important when plants that like to be cool are in hot rooms.

Indoor plants respond to frequent showers by displaying fresh greenery and good color. Showers keep plants clean and healthy, taking the place of the rain that provided baths, weekly or more often, when plants were growing outdoors.

Houseplants That Summer Outdoors

Houseplants that have summered outdoors benefit enormously from their months in the fresh air, but they need the same treatment when brought in as do outdoor plants moved indoors. Avocado, ficus and African violets really flourish during summer vacation, and will find the shock of their return inside less debilitating if they are given lots of fresh air and moisture. One plant does differ a little: The African violet doesn't respond well to misting, though it likes to be rinsed gently with a fine spray of lukewarm water about once a month. After misting, let the leaves dry in semishade—don't set wet leaves in direct sun or the violet will suffer.

Houseplants that have summered outside may bring white flies back indoors with them. Somehow, they seem affected very little by white flies when they are outdoors, especially if they are in an airy corner. But when they are put back inside, where there are no breezes to keep the pests from settling in quantity on the plants, there are problems.

Before you bring the plants back in, spray them for several weeks before the move. Once they are inside, mist and shower often until all signs of white flies are gone. Some household pesticides offer white fly control.

Consider repotting. Houseplants placed outdoors usually grow much more quickly than when they are living indoors. Your plants will look great by summer's end, but they may need new soil and a larger pot to live in. For repotting information, see page 74.

An Overnight Herb Garden

You can create an herb garden right in your house by digging up the herbs growing in your outdoor garden. The fact that many of the herbs we normally grow outdoors will flourish indoors provides a new perspective on what we normally consider planting outdoors. Some of the lovely perennial herbs that are usually treated as annuals (because the winter cold kills them) become good garden subjects when you know that you

Pots of herbs, fingertip fresh, thrive in a sunny window. To perk up the arrangement, bring in sun-loving annuals from the garden.

Tree-form rosemary

can winter them indoors. Lemon-verbena is a good example.

Some of the winter-hardy herbs (thyme, for example), which become inaccessible when they are covered with snow, should be brought in, too.

Indoors, many herbs will succeed on a windowsill where they have a few hours of direct sunlight daily. Other herbs will do better in a fluorescent-light garden. As a matter of fact, most herbs do well under fluorescent light, but some of those you pot up to bring in may be too big for your flourescent-light garden.

The garden herbs you pot and bring indoors are handled somewhat differently from those you start from seed. Outdoor herbs, like country mice, won't acclimatize to sophisticated living conditions, so it's up to you to provide them with indoor conditions that resemble their outdoor situation as closely as possible.

This thinking governs the choice of containers and soil. For herbs that will be brought indoors, I prefer the porous clay pots. Rosemary and basil are the exceptions. They seem to be in such trouble if they dry out in the pot that I grow them in plastic pots, which hold moisture longer than clay pots.

Because herbs growing indoors face much drier conditions than they did outdoors, they need a soil that holds moisture well. Herbs generally come from environments where the soil is on the sandy side; when grown outdoors, most are more successful in sandy garden loam. Indoors, when grown from seed, they do best in all-purpose soil, which holds moisture a little better than sandy garden loam. However, it's been my experience that an outdoor plant that was thriving in garden loam will be happier if it remains in the same kind of soil. So, when I pot herbs to bring indoors, I pot them in soil dug from the spot in which they were growing. I dig up as much of the root balls as I conveniently can, and I put them in the roomiest container that I can manage so there's plenty of soil should they wish to grow new roots.

Since herbs do require good drainage, I place a layer of small pebbles 2 to 3 inches deep on the bottom of the container before adding the soil. Herbs usually have fairly compact root balls. Set the ball into the pot before you add the soil. Scratch a mark at the level at which the ball must be placed to bring the crown (where the stems meet the roots) of the plant 1 to 2 inches below the pot rim. Add soil to the mark, place the root ball on the soil and fill with soil to the crown.

When you are potting perennial herbs, like the tree-form rosemary in the illustration at left, choose a good-size container, since the plant will live in it for a long time.

Care of Herbs Moved Indoors

The handling suggestions for herbs (see pages 36–40) apply generally to the herbs you bring in as well as to those you grow indoors from seed. However, herbs you bring in are accustomed to fresh air and moisture in a way that herbs which are born indoors are not. Keep the brought-in herbs in a cool spot or air the room they grow in often. Misting often is particularly important in the beginning and should be continued at regular intervals later on.

Herbs to Bring In

Although most herbs will, in theory, succeed indoors, the herbs I've had most luck bringing in are these: basil, sweet bay, chives, parsley, rosemary, sage, tarragon, lemon-verbena and thyme. Some of these are easy to grow from seed in early spring or late winter, and then set outdoors when the warm weather comes. You can buy others as seedlings at garden supply centers in spring.

Basil: You can grow both ordinary green and decorative purple basil from seed. Pinched at the tip often during the summer, they will stay compact and make attractive plants to dig for indoor growing in the fall. I think the purple varieties are pretty in the garden, but I prefer the green for flavoring. Pot several plants together in a big container, cut the tops back by a third and install on a sunny sill or under fluorescents. Don't let the soil dry out. Mist often. If white flies appear, shower often and increase the mistings.

Bay, sweet: Sweet bay is a very attractive evergreen houseplant. Buy young plants in spring, grow them in the garden in their pots for summer and bring them indoors in

fall. A sunny east or west window provides enough light. Keep the soil evenly moist. Use leaves at will for flavoring—but beware—I have found the flavor of the fresh leaf in this herb more pungent than the flavor of dried leaves. The reverse is true with most herbs.

Chives: These can be started from seed in early spring, set outdoors and left over the winter since they are hardy. So, dig up only half the clump to pot for a winter indoors. Keep chives, whether growing indoors or outdoors, picked free of flowers. The flowers are edible, and they make pretty toppings for summer salads. Keep chives cut, (use the cuttings for flavoring) to keep them growing. If your plant begins to look withered, with yellowed stems showing, divide and repot each half in fresh soil. Keep it moist, but not too wet, until growth begins, then water regularly. Grow chives in a sunny window.

Geranium, scented-leaf: This wonderful houseplant is usually purchased as a seedling in the spring,

set out for summer and brought in for winter. Like other geraniums, the scented types are not hardy in the cold regions. Brought indoors in fall (see page 6), they will grow in a few years into giant potted plants that give off a wonderful spicy fragrance when their leaves are touched. There are many scents or flavors—rose, mint, orange, apple—but usually only a few scents are available locally. It's best to take what you find until you come across one you really want. The scented-leaf geraniums propagate easily from tip cuttings in spring—so you can make duplicates for friends. Rose-scented types make very nice Christmas presents for friends who preserve, since the leaves are often called for in old recipes.

Marjoram, sweet: Sweet marjoram can be started from seed indoors in spring, summered outdoors and brought back indoors in fall. It makes a pretty houseplant if kept in a sunny spot or under fluorescents and pinched back often. The flavor is similar to that of oregano.

Sweet bay

Thyme

Lemon-verbena

Some plants sold as oregano are, in fact, sweet marjoram. Be sure the soil is kept evenly moist. Mist the plant often, as it is subject to red spider-mite, a pest that thrives in stale, hot, dry air. Sweet marjoram is a perennial and should go on for years if conditions are right.

Mint: Mint is fun to bring indoors, even though it is difficult to keep up for more than a few months. Seedlings grow fairly well under fluorescent lights. Buy young plants in early spring and set out in their containers. Unless the roots are confined by a pot, mint tends to take over the whole garden. Divide plant in fall, leaving half in its container in the ground. Though your indoor plant may die eventually, you'll have plenty left outdoors for next year.

Oregano: See Marjoram, sweet.

Parsley: This is the herb I use most. I sow a whole row outdoors in spring and bring in two or three big clumps in fall. These will usually last on a cool, sunny window for several months. Before Christmas, I start a batch of parsley seedlings (see page 39), snip them to keep the plants compact and my kitchen supplied during late winter and spring. These plants are set out in spring to supply summer needs. Parsley is a biennial, and it goes to seed the second year, so the original row is pretty well gone by the time the new planting has taken hold.

Rosemary: Start from seed (see page 39) and summer the seedlings outdoors. Pot up in fall and bring indoors to a cool room and

A strawberry jar of perennial herbs preserves summertime flavor and fragrance during winter months. Trim back and summer outdoors.

a sunny window, or try it under fluorescents. Pruned to a tree shape, it becomes a delightful houseplant. It's an evergreen perennial and will go on for years, once acclimatized.

Sage: Sage can be started from seed indoors and summered outdoors. In fall, dig a healthy clump, and prune the branches back severely before bringing it indoors to a sunny window or, preferably, fluorescents. Keep tips pinched back.

Tarragon: Buy seedlings in spring, summer outdoors and bring inside in the fall. Tarragon won't last forever. It needs a "winter," or chilling period, which you can give it if the plant begins to look tacky. Place outdoors on a sill or in the refrigerator for a month. Start new plants from tip cuttings in spring.

Thyme: Thyme is a hardy perennial that can be grown from seed or purchased as a started seedling. It roots easily from tip cuttings, too, so you can multiply your holdings every spring if you wish. Place it in a sunny window indoors. Thyme can be grown as a basket plant, the branches allowed to cascade. Cool, fresh air is important to keep the plant attractive, and tips must be pinched back regularly. Mist often. Allow to dry slightly between waterings.

Lemon-verbena: Lemon-verbena is usually purchased as a seedling and grown as a container plant on the patio. In warm regions, it grows big and is evergreen. In cool regions, it often loses its leaves in winter and stays rather small. Bring indoors in winter in its container if temperatures in your area go as low as 20 degrees above zero. Place in direct sun and keep soil evenly moist. Mist often and air

the room as frequently as you can. It can stand quite a lot of heat, but dry air combined with dried out soil can be fatal.

Bring In Wildlings

At almost every time of the year, even in winter, woodlands and roadsides offer many charming big and little plants you can bring indoors. Avoid the wildlings that are protected by your state. I can't list them because each state has its own special list of plants to cherish. Many wild plants are not protected, so the choice is enormous. Not all will live forever. Those growing in terrariums and bottle gardens can go on for years and years, but most will live for several weeks to several months, sometimes longer if handled carefully. I still remember with delight the clump of bright yellow marsh marigolds I dug from a roadside swamp one year. It bloomed for weeks in an old aquarium tank. And I have often brought in the little *Hepatica acutiloba,* which blooms early in dry areas of the woods.

Children especially love woodland rambles to find wild plants. They are wonderful at spotting the exquisite, strangely colored fungi that push up from leaf mold, and they love collecting leaf mold, mosses, acorns, rocks, lichens and tiny ferns for planting and decorating your terrariums and bottle garden projects.

The elements of the forest floor are the natural habitat of the wildlings, and to transplant them successfully to your indoor garden you must bring in soil from their growing spots with the plants. Tiny twigs, pebbles, gravel and mosses from the environment they called home add charm to the containers they grow in.

The terrarium and the bottle garden operate on the same principles: They are glass enclosed, so they preserve and reuse their oxygen and water supplies; they demand little attention from the gardener who created them; they make handsome garden pieces for any area of the house. If you chose plants from the forest floor, they will be happiest in low-lighting.

Digging Ferns and Other Wild Plants

The best time to transplant wildlings is in the early growing days of spring. Dig them before noon heat, or well after midday sun, and when the soil is damp, not soggy wet. Dig as big a root ball as you can with each plant. Since truly giant soil clumps are hard to keep intact, it is wise to limit the size of your choices. Remember, too, younger plants adapt more easily to a changed environment than do mature plants.

The procedure for digging a wild fern is typical of the procedure for digging any small plant. First, spade a circle all around the plant, well outside the perimeter of its foliage. Next, dig straight down along the circle line to cleanly cut any outlying roots. Then, push your spade, angled toward the plant, (I use a spading fork, which I find easier) into the ground, and lift gently. Lift all around the circle until you sense the roots are free.

Transplanting bush- and tree-size plants requires planning. The basic procedure is the same, but two stages are involved. In order for the plant to reestablish any cut roots, it should be left where it is for several weeks or even a whole season. Prepare the plant on the first trip. If you push burlap or plastic into the soil around the root ball, you'll encourage the plant to form new roots within the root ball, and when the time comes to transplant, it will have a head start. At that time, lift the plant onto a burlap bag. Be careful to break the root ball as little as possible. Bring home as much soil as you will need to fill your container. You will use this as potting soil. (Pasteurize it, as described on page 76). When you get home, pot

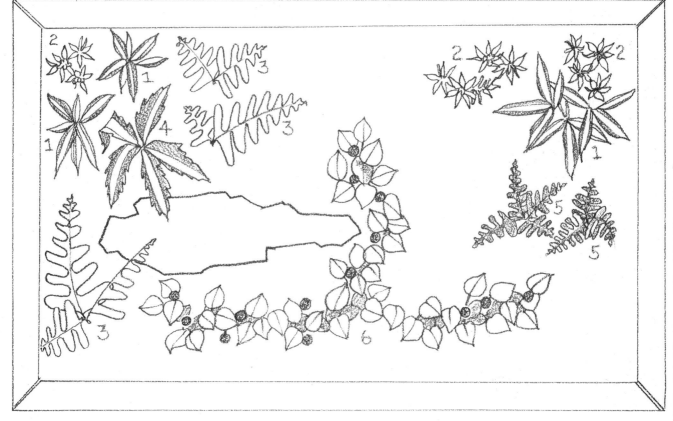

Planting plan for terrarium pictured on page 16 (as seen from above): 1. spotted wintergreen; 2. shining clubmoss; 3. common polypody; 4. pipsissewa; 5. ebony spleenwort; 6. partridgeberry.

Layer chips, charcoal and soil.

the plant (see page 73). Let it rest
for a few days outdoors, in a light
similar to that in which it grew,
before you bring it in to its permanent home. Keep the soil evenly
moist for most woodland plants,
and mist often the first weeks of
indoor life. To keep the plant
healthy and attractive, remove
any dead branches or leaves as
soon as they appear.

Place the plant in light as similar
to the kind it grew in in the woods
as possible, and keep an eye on its
progress. If the branches reach upward with pale leaves sparsely
spaced along them, chances are
there's not enough light. If leaves
show browning, burned or bronzed
areas, or turn a sickly yellow-green,
chances are there is too much direct sunlight.

Although these instructions do
describe handling large plants,
the same procedure applies to
digging and handling small plants
—it's just a lot easier.

Plants for a
Woodland Terrarium
When you are looking for woodland plants for a terrarium, keep in
mind the fact that you are going to
transplant them to a humid environment. Mosses, lichens and
such won't present a problem, but

plants dug in dry, sandy areas
won't be happy in humid terrariums. A rather dimly lighted, moist
area of the woods is the best place
to look for terrarium and bottle
garden plants.

Not all the things you will want
to grow in terrariums and bottle
gardens come from the wild. A
terrarium is an ideal place to nur-
ture some of the moisture-loving
houseplants you may want to
propagate. A bit of color is especially welcome in these enclosed
gardens—the bloom of a miniature
African violet or a miniature
gloxinia (Sinningia pusilla), for
instance. These and other plants are
available from miniature-plant
dealers. When I've nothing blooming in a terrarium, I sometimes pick
a bright blossom from a large
houseplant, poke it into a tiny vial
of water and bury it in the terrarium
in a spot that highlights its color.

If you want a few exotic accents
in your garden, growers and nurser-
ies specializing in miniatures offer
selaginellas, mosslike perennials,
annuals from warm regions and
miniature varieties of cypress,
spruce, hemlock, yew and fir. Small
pileas and peperomias are also available. Miniature aluminum plant,
miniature peperomia (a pilea),
watermelon peperomia and 'Emer-
ald Ripple' are popular.

Miniature plants are so popular
that many of the best-known plants
are now cultivated in this form.
Sinningia pusilla, mentioned earlier, is the smallest moisture-loving
plant I know. In a covered container it blooms nonstop on a
stem as slender as a needle. The
miniature begonias, ivies and
orchids are other possibilities.
Low-growing ground covers add
charm to both terrariums and bottle gardens. Among my favorites
are baby's tears and tiny strawberry geraniums, which creep over

Position tallest plants first.

the ground and have exquisite
foliage.

Plants for terrariums and bottle
gardens require similar growing
conditions; however, small plants
are grown in terrariums—slightly
taller plants in the bottle gardens.
For terrariums, seek out baby
maidenhair ferns; rock ferns; rat-
tlesnake ferns, which have criss-
crossed white veins on their
leaves; ebony spleenwort, which
loves shade; oak fern; birdsnest
fern; holly fern; Victorian fern; and
the button fern, whose round
leaves and dark stems make it
ornamental and very interesting.

Containers for Terrariums
Florists and garden centers sell
terrariums of all sorts—brandy snif-
ters, mushroom-shaped glassware
terrariums, globes, bowls. You can
economize by looking for a container among your stored discards:
fish tanks and bowls, vases and
other glass treasures. The material
has to be clear glass or plastic so
that you can see the miniature
terrain you create. The humid terrariums need lids. If necessary,
have a glass sheet cut to fit by a
hardware store. It won't cost
much. You can also use a trans-
parent dish or saucer as a lid.

Planting a Terrarium

To duplicate the terrarium on page 16, you will need a glass bowl with an 8-inch opening. Start the terrarium by adding 1 inch of marble chips or tiny, washed river pebbles to the bottom for drainage. Next, add 2 to 3 cups of moist bagged terrarium soil. Or make your own mixture: equal parts of bagged all-purpose potting soil, sand (or perlite), vermiculite, ground sphagnum peat moss and charcoal chips. I recommend that you use one of the commercial mixes, or make your own of bagged components. All of these are pasteurized and free of harmful fungi that may grow in unpasteurized soils. I know this sounds like a contradiction of my earlier suggestion that you plant your wildlings in the soil they came from. To clarify: I suggest forest soil for larger plants that will grow in open air, pasteurized soils for the smaller plants that will go into a covered terrarium where the humidity is constant.

After the soil has been added, shape it into a little landscape with your fingers. Raise some areas and lower others. Plan where the terrarium will be displayed and how the light will hit it. Then mold a terrain that will show the plants well in the chosen location.

Unpot your plants and set the tallest in first. Scoop a little planting hole in the soil, press the root ball into position and gently firm the soil with your hands until the plant stands upright. Add the smaller plants next, and arrange the ground covers last. When all

---

Want a special decoration for a child's room? Try a terrarium. It is almost carefree and can be lit with real or artificial light.

the plants are firmly in place, you may want to scatter a little more soil loosely over the ground to level bumpy spots. Then place wood moss (you can gather the wood moss in the wild or you can buy it in sheets at garden supply centers) over the soil, and add a tiny white birch twig and a pretty rock, or whatever accessories strike your fancy. Add just enough water to settle the roots into place. The water fills minute air pockets and, when it runs down into the drainage pebbles, draws soil in around the roots. Don't overwater—you'll drown everything. Cover the terrarium.

For its first few days, set the terrarium in rather dim light. Then move it to its permanent home near, but not in, direct sun. Or set it under fluorescent lights.

I've emphasized woodland terrariums because we are dealing primarily with wild plants to bring in, but miniature desertscapes are also popular terrariums. However, these require sand instead of humusy soil, cacti and succulents instead of moisture-loving plants, and they are left uncovered.

The planting plan on page 14 shows which plants were used to create the terrarium on page 16.

Consider a Bottle Garden

A bottle garden is an exquisite landscape in miniature. In a dark corner, under fluorescents, it lights up the whole area. A really good one is a living, breathing painting.

The bottle garden on page 21 was planted in a hand-blown glass container, and doubles its interest by the use of form and color in the drainage layers of charcoal, pebbles and sand at the bottom. But a bottle garden needn't be this size, and it can be planted in an inexpensive con-

tainer. Some of the miniature plants described on the preceding page as suited to a woodland terrarium make adorable little landscapes that can be planted in discarded apothecary, candy or cookie jars. A single *Sinningia pusilla* with a bit of moss at its feet, blooming in a tiny cast-off vitamin pill bottle, makes a mini-mini-bottle garden which shows up beautifully if well lighted. Big pickling jars in quart sizes can be used as bottle gardens, as can gallon cider jugs. Most canning jars are boring, but now and again you run across an old-fashioned jar or an imported one that is quite handsome in its stark simplicity.

I suggest you try your very first bottle garden in a container you have handy, and if you enjoy this project, search the glass shops, five-and-dime stores, secondhand and antique stores for a truly handsome glass shape in which to plant a more ambitious garden. One of the prettiest bottle gardens I've ever seen was planted in an old water-cooler jug.

Equipment for Planting a Bottle Garden

There's nothing miraculous about the way in which the plants get into a bottle garden. It's done with a rolled-up cylinder of newspaper. But to make and keep a bottle garden, you do need some equipment. You already may have, or can improvise, most or all of it.

Syringe: You will need some sort of fine spraying equipment to clear off the inside of the bottle after planting. Cleaning up the container is one of the most finicky aspects of making a bottle garden beautiful. A bulb baster for roasts is ideal for the job. A rubber shower spray attachment, minus the shower head, will work if the water is turned very low so that only a little water trickles out.

Poker: Not a fireplace poker, but a long, rather pointed instrument with a blunt end for poking. A big chopstick will do, or simply a long piece of wood about 1 inch wide at one end and ¼ to ½ inch around at the other end. The length needed depends on the size of the bottle.

Long-handled paintbrush: The brush helps remove dust and dirt from the plants and from the sides of the bottle.

Wooden tongs: These also help clean up the sides of the jar. Primarily used to dig planting holes, tongs are especially handy for maneuvering roots into the holes.

Funnel: This is a help in getting soil into a small bottle—but there are other ways. The rolled-up cylinder of newspaper makes a good funnel for a large bottle.

In addition to these garden helpers, a mechanic's pickup tool is recommended for maintenance chores. It permits you to pick up small objects in places where your hand won't fit. Another aid is a long stick with a safety-razor blade attached to one end used to prune branches as the plants grow.

Materials for Planting a Bottle Garden

The materials used in a bottle garden are essentially the same as those used in planting a terrarium. Be sure to include moss. If you want to make a bottle garden with many colorful levels, in addition to gravel, charcoal chips and terrarium potting soil, you will need sand and some of those sparkling white marble chips in small sizes.

The sand used in gardening of any sort must be free of salt; not sea sand, in other words. Garden

Planting plan for bottle garden pictured on page 21: 1. palm; 2. English ivy; 3. golden baby's tears; 4. creeping fig; 5. strawberry begonia; 6. Irish moss.

supply centers sell "sharp sand" with jagged surfaces that allow for very good drainage. Sharp sand is mixed into potting soils and can be used in terrariums. I find the sand employed in sand paintings too fine to be used in big bottle gardens. Without the air spaces created by the sharp sand's jagged edges, sand lies inert and holds too much water for good drainage. It's all right for little desertscapes. They are pretty on top of sand paintings in bottles, but big bottle gardens layered several inches deep in humusy terrarium soil need the kind of sand that really drains well.

You can use sea sand for gardening if you are willing to wash it for hours until you are sure it is free of salt. If you need only a small quantity, then that is a reasonable undertaking. If you need a lot—a bagful, for instance—for mixing with your potting soil, then washing sand would be a nightmare.

Collecting pebbles to layer the bottom of a bottle garden is another of those "collecting" projects that children adore. And there are so many pretty pebbles lying around that the collecting doesn't take forever. Wash the stones well.

Plants for a Bottle Garden

Since the really handsome bottle gardens are the big ones, here are some suggestions for plants (up to about 12 inches tall) suitable for this size:

Dragon lily
  Dracaena godseffiana,
    'Florida Beauty'
English ivy, miniature
  Hedera helix
Fan maidenhair fern
  Adiantum tenerum 'Wrightii'
Firecracker flower
  Crossandra
Flame violet
  Episcia reptans, 'Lady Lou'
Grape-ivy, miniature
  Cissus rhombifolia
Jewel orchid
  Anoectochilus
Mexican foxglove
  Allophyton mexicanum
Mosaic plant
  Fittonia verschaffeltii
Philodendron, silver-leaf (when
    very small)
  Philodendron sodiroi
Prayer plant (when very small)
  Maranta
Sweet flag, miniature
  Acorus gramineus variegatus
Variegated Sedge, miniature
  Carex
Venus fly-trap
  Dionaea muscipula
Victorian table fern
  Pteris ensiformis 'Victoriae'

Any number of baby houseplants can start out in a bottle garden, as long as you are willing to transplant them when they out-

grow their home. But these must be moisture-loving plants that thrive in high humidity, and they should be plants that grow very slowly, or you'll be transplanting gangling growers every other week. A bottle garden spurs growth.

Miniatures and dwarfs, by the way, don't always stay the size they are when you buy them. They are usually young plants when sold to you and will grow larger. The *Sinningia pusilla* is one that won't —it is tiny and stays tiny. But most others eventually outgrow their homes. However, they'll take longer to do it than will standard-size plants.

Preparing a Bottle

The very first step in making a bottle garden is to clean the container. Wash it thoroughly inside and outside with water and detergent. If there are stubborn spots or filmed areas on the inside (as there sometimes are in old bottles), fill the bottle with a strong

Use rolled-up newspaper to funnel the materials into the bottle.

Layered materials provide drainage as well as form and color in bottles.

solution of ammonia and water. If this doesn't do the trick, pour out most of the ammonia solution, then pour small pebbles (about ½ cup) into the bottle and shake hard.

Rinse the bottle thoroughly, especially if you have used ammonia. Now you must get the inside dry, or the soil and other materials that you pour in will cake the insides of the jar, cling to the moist areas and make cleaning up after planting a tedious job. I use my hair blower to dry the inside. The air vent of the vacuum cleaner will do the same job. If water spots remain, you might try washing the bottle again with one of the water-spot removers used in the dishwasher. You can then clasp bunched-up paper towels in tongs and wipe the inside dry.

Cleaning the bottle is tedious, but the beauty of a bottle garden is lost unless the container is sparkling clean. To shine the outside of the bottle, I use window-cleaning spray and polish with paper towels.

Adding the Soil
With the bottle shiny clean and perfect, you are ready to put in the planting materials. Pour the drainage materials and soil into the bottle through a funnel made of newspaper. If it is a small container, pour through a regular funnel. The drainage materials should be dry. The terrarium soil may be a little damp, but not really moist. Begin with a layer of pebbles, pea gravel or marble chips. If you are planting in a small bottle garden, 1 to 2 inches should be enough. If you are planting in a big bottle, and plan to show off many layers of drainage materials at the bottom, then add enough of this layer to fill up one-eighth to one-quarter of the bottom. Create hills

and valleys—don't level the surface. If the bottle is to have display layers, a screen of cut-up colorless nylon stocking laid over the top of each will keep the materials from sifting together and will make more sharply defined layers.

The next level is a layer of charcoal chips. If the bottle is small, 1 inch of charcoal is enough. If the bottle is large, 2 inches is about right. Add this layer so that it covers the hills and valleys of marble chips to make a contrasting dark line.

If you are planting in a small bottle, the next layer should then be terrarium soil; but if you are making a work of art of the layers, then the next level should be sand. Sand is quite dusty, so pour it slowly and keep the pouring end of the rolled-up paper as close to the bottom of the bottle as possible. Cover the hills and valleys of the previous layer, and when that is complete, add more sand, about half the depth of the marble chips. Pour it so that the hills are over the valleys of the marble chips, and the valleys are over the hills. The bottle should be about one-third full when this is done. Next, add terrarium soil until the bottle is half full.

Whether for a big bottle or a small one, shape the terrarium soil into different levels so that tall plants will show off well but will not hide the tiny plants.

Planting a Bottle Garden
Make a planting plan for your garden. Set out and look over the plants you have chosen. Outline the bottom of the bottle on a sheet of newspaper with a crayon and arrange the plants on it attractively. You may want to readjust the dips and valleys of terrarium soil to feature certain plants. With the crayon, circle each pot bottom on the

newspaper and write in the name of the plant, so you won't forget or lose your plan halfway through planting.

The next step is to unpot the biggest plant. To unpot a plant, rap the pot edge sharply on the edge of the sink. Flip the pot over with your fingers stretched over the soil, and the root ball should slide out into your hand. Remove most of the soil from around the plant roots. Shaking will free some of the soil, and more soil will come away if you rinse the root gently under a spray of lukewarm water. Some soil will still cling to the roots—and that's all right. Tuck the plant into the corner of a small sheet of newspaper, a sheet only as long as the plant is tall. Roll it up gently so that you don't crush the leaves, but firmly enough to make a cone that will slide through the bottle neck. Keep your planting plan in mind, and with the tongs slide the plant into the bottle. Release it as close to its planting site as possible. Use the tongs to shake the plant free of paper, then pull the paper back out. With the tongs or poker, scoop out a little planting hole, lift the plant into the planting hole and set it upright. This takes a little maneuvering, so be patient and gentle. I find that if I get a good grip on the roots at just the right angle, I can lift them and press them into the planting hole in such a way that the plant stays more or less upright. Then, by pressing the roots a little deeper into the soil, I can get the plant to stand straight. After that, it is easy to push more soil in around the roots and firm it.

A bottle garden is an elegant work of art. With proper lighting, its setting can change to suit your decorating needs or mood.

When the plant is standing at just the right angle, add the next largest plant.

As you add each plant, the terrain changes a little, and the planting plan may also change somewhat. Keep in mind the place where the bottle will be displayed. Will you always see it at the same angle, or will you want to look at it from all sides? This affects the final arrangement of the plants. Will it be under fluorescent lights? Will it have to be turned often to face the light source?

Cleaning Up the Project
When all the plants are in the bottle, it is time to groom your garden. Begin by cleaning up the plants. As they land on the soil surface, leaves and flowers pick up some dirt. Using the long-handled paintbrush, dust the plants. Use the poker to free caught limbs and leaves. Rake the tongs over the soil to smooth the surface; add little pieces of forest moss or moss from the florist to carpet the floor of your garden. Poke these into place and firm them gently into the soil. Add stones, shells and twigs to finish the composition.

Rinse the leaves clean, one by one. If you are using a hose, turn the water very, very low—a trickle is all you need. Control the flow of water by pinching the hose. The less water you pour in for each part of the cleanup job, the less likely the bottle is to be water logged. Dribble water on the inside walls to clear away specks of dirt and dust.

Care of a
Terrarium or Bottle Garden
If light, moisture and temperature are in good balance in your glass garden, it will last for years.

The right light for most bottle gardens and terrariums is bright daylight. Direct sun is generally

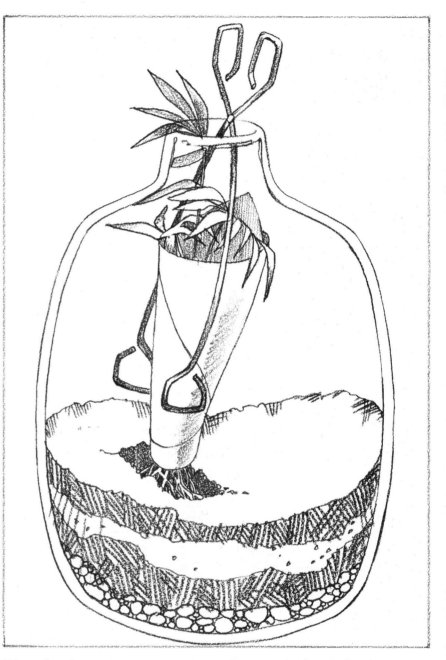

Wrap plant in newspaper; use tongs to insert each plant in bottle; use tongs to unwrap and position the plant.

not desirable. Bright light means a few feet to either side of a sunny east, west or south window. Light also may be supplied by a bright north window.

If you are using fluorescent fixtures to light your garden, place them over the bottle and turn them on for 14 to 16 hours a day in the beginning. Raise or lower them according to the plant's responses. If plant leaves begin to brown, the lights may be too close. If they begin to yellow and reach upward, more light is needed —so place the lights closer to the plants, or the plants closer to the lights. If that doesn't do the trick,

Use tongs to set and secure plant.

leave them on an hour or two longer. I suggest you use a standard fluorescent fixture with two 20-watt or two 40-watt bulbs, one Daylight, the other Warm White.

Covered terrariums and bottle gardens require very little watering; about every two or three weeks is enough. Overwatered, they'll die. Signs of overwatering are mold and big beads of water inside the glass.

Check the garden for symptoms of water need. A covered terrarium or bottle garden usually has very fine beads of moisture—a mist, really—on its glass sides and top. As long as you can see moisture, there is enough moisture for the plants. When there is no moisture whatsoever on the inside of the glass, then it probably needs watering. You will find that when you want to really show off your garden, you must remove the top for a few minutes to let the moisture on the glass dry.

Another symptom of water need is wilted leaves, or leaves that appear a dull green. For a 4-quart bottle, spray ½ cup of water over the greenery. If the garden still looks dull the next day, add another ½ cup of water.

Grooming the garden is important not only for appearance but also to keep the garden healthy. Rotting vegetation may lead to disease. Remove any yellowing or faded leaves on the plants and on the garden floor. This is where a mechanic's pickup tool is helpful. When leaves must be cut from branches, slice them free with the corner of a safety-razor blade, then fish them out with the mechanic's pickup tool.

Feed terrariums and bottle gardens twice yearly. You want the plants to stay within the size of their containers. Use a liquid foliage-plant fertilizer at half strength.

Check the container occasionally for dying plants. Although most of the plants suggested generally do well in containers, not all plants adjust to their changed environments. If a plant dies, remove it with tongs. You may find the other plants in the container have grown and that the container actually looks better without a replacement.

Find a Wild Plant to Make a Bonsai

With a carefully selected wild plant, you can create a wonderful little living sculpture—a bonsai. Bonsai appeals to many beginning gardeners, and it is a project of quality rather than quantity. To buy a bonsai costs a great deal because of the time required to achieve a mature plant. It's a good project for the economy-minded because, in time, it will provide a valuable plant from very humble sources.

Bonsai means "tray arrangement." The plant used in a bonsai is a miniature or dwarfed plant trained to the dramatic shape that nature sometimes carves in wild or rocky places. To find a suitable

Tape razor blade to stick to prune.

bonsai subject, search in fields and along cliffs where growth is the opposite of lush. Look in your own or a friend's garden and at the local greenhouse for plants that are misshapen and a disgrace to the landscape. Starved, cramped roots and big winds are nature's tools for making full-scale bonsai subjects.

Let me emphasize here that I am not going to tell you how to make a true, prize-winning, classical bonsai. It is a ceremonious art, heavy with tradition, and neither you nor I could explore it in these pages.

Plants for a Bonsai

Flowering shrubs, tropical plants and trees that will live indoors are suitable for bonsai, and collectors use them. For the beginner, the most attractive bonsai on a year 'round basis are broadleaved or needled evergreens. Some good subjects are Japanese boxwood, atlas cedar, sawara cypress, rockspray, perny holly, Enlish-ivy, Chinese juniper, Western red cedar, sheep laurel, jack pine, mugho pine, firethorn, weeping hemlock and the common forest evergreens of North America.

Spruce is typical. Avoid wild plants with tap roots (a single carrotlike main root) since they don't like to be root pruned.

In selecting specimens, look for a bold and dramatically different structure of stem and branches. Consider what the basic shape will be with some twigs and side branches removed.

Soil and Equipment for a Bonsai

Bonsai soil, almost devoid of loam, is a mixture of clay (or Terra Green or Turface, commercial products), sand and humus. Experts make their own, but the beginner will do best with commercially bagged bonsai soil. The basic composition is simulated by mixing equal parts of sandy garden loam, sphagnum peat moss and coarse perlite. Do not use soil that offers timed release fertilizers. Bonsai, like bottle gardens, require very little feeding. You are dwarfing plants, not growing a forest.

The container a bonsai grows in is its frame. There are traditional container shapes designed for specific types of bonsai. I suggest you find the plant first, and then look for a container that will balance harmoniously the size and proposed final shape of your project. Glazed pottery bonsai containers in red, mustard, blue and green are sold by garden supply centers and many five-and-dime stores. They usually are rectangular, circular or oval in shape and shallow, deliberately so, to restrict growth.

Tools you'll need are small pruning shears, a poker, chopsticks for cleaning roots and medium-gauge wire. A bit of mesh to screen the drainage holes will help, and you will want fine moss to finish the surface. Pretty stones add to the composition, too.

You also will need very low-growing, fine moss. You probably can find the right kind in the woods, growing on rocks in damp places where the light is rather dim. Collect the moss in sheets in a plastic bag with a little water in it. Keep it moist until you are ready to use it to cover the soil surface of your bonsai plant.

Starting a Bonsai

The first step in the bonsai process is to acclimatize your subject. Whether it's a wild plant you've dug up (see page 23) or a greenhouse special, transplant it to a standard pot and place it in subdued light until it shows new growth, a sign that it has established itself. (In spring, this will probably take a few weeks.) Then you can begin the shaping process. Set yourself up in the kitchen. Have equipment and soil handy and work on big sheets of newspaper. Unpot the plant and shake the soil away from the root system until all the main roots are clearly visible. Now, lift the plant into its home container. Estimate how much root has to be removed to allow the plant to fit the container. The upper portions of the

Broken lines show pruning steps to clear the first and the second third of the wildling bonsai trunk.

roots—where the roots meet the trunk—should be raised above the container. This will create the desired effect of a gnarly rooted old tree.

Cover the container drainage holes with squares of mesh and secure them with tape. Cut a piece of florist's wire about 36 inches long. Thread it through the drainage holes and the mesh up into the pot and out at either end. The wires will be used to secure the plant.

Planting a Bonsai

You are now ready to plant. Pour about ½ inch of damp-to-moist soil into the container and set the tree on it. Usually a bonsai is placed off-center. The key word is asymmetry. Walk all around the plant and decide which is its best angle. Turn the tree in the container until you are satisfied that it is displayed to its best advantage. You may have to prune a few more roots but don't go overboard. Try to see the plant as a picturesque, old tree you are viewing from half a mile away. Think-

ing of the bonsai's ultimate form is the fun of bonsai work, and ideas for shapes develop only as you think about the tree and look for inspiration. Eventually you will prune away more branches and wire others into shape. Make sure the top portion of the roots at the base of the trunk are showing above the container rim, since these are part of your composition. Take your time, but don't take so long that the roots begin to dry out. If this should happen, you can sprinkle a little water over them.

The next step is to prune away any limbs growing from the lower third of the tree. From the middle third of the tree (the center) remove front branches. Only the side and back limbs should remain —the front should be bare. The top third of the tree usually has limbs all around. Take these instructions only as guidelines. Yours may be a specimen of twisted pine with strikingly structured branching that should be thinned only in the top two thirds. You may have a different idea from seeing other

bonsai—follow it. This is your bonsai, and it should be fun!

To firm the tree in place, cross the ends of the wires over the trunk, twist them together, then bury them under the root mass. Cut a piece of medium-gauge wire about 5 feet long. Slip one end of the wire under the root mass; pull it through until the wire is centered. Bring the two ends together, make a single wire and wrap this in a spiral up the trunk to the most important side branch. Separate the two wires and spiral-wrap the side branch with one. Spiral-wrap the remaining wire up the trunk to the top of the tree. Then use the wrapped wire to lead the trunk and main branch in directions best suited for your composition.

You can't make the tree turn a right angle, but by bending it slightly and holding it in place with the wire over a period of time, you can slant it until it is growing almost at right angles, if that is what you want. Use medium-gauge wire wrapped in spirals around the other main branches if you wish to improve

Line bottom of tray with wire mesh and push wires through drainage holes (left); after planting, wire trunk and main branch (middle); then wire the secondary branches to complete shaping (right).

the growing direction of these branches.

Cut away wire ends that are too long. You don't want sharp things poking out from your bonsai. After several months of training, the branches will be growing in the right direction, and unless a given branch needs more training, the wire can be removed. When the trunk has acquired a direction and is obviously growing in it, you can remove the wire from the trunk, too. The wires are temporary training measures.

Next, add moist, not soaking, soil to the container, right to the rim. You may find the composition more attractive if there is soil piled a little above the rim in some spots, usually near the base of the trunk. Make a slight depression in the soil just inside the container rim, to hold water.

As you add the soil, use the poker to eliminate air pockets and to bring the soil into close contact with the roots.

Many bonsai have irregularities in the landscape of the soil surface to suggest the undulations natural to the terrain in which such a tree might grow. You can experiment with this idea and see what it does for the planting. Irregularity adds interest to the soil surface.

Remove enough of the soil at the bottom of the main trunk to expose the plant's heavy roots. An artist's brush is a good tool to do this with, if you have one handy, or a soft-bristled toothbrush will do just as well.

Place the plant in the kitchen sink and shower it thoroughly with lukewarm water. It has gone through a lot and needs reviving. Allow the container to drain one to two hours. Before you place the bonsai in its permanent home, cover the soil surface with moss. First soak the moss in a bowl of lukewarm water for 10 to 15 minutes.

Care of a Bonsai

The major maintenance problem in caring for a bonsai is the watering. This is one plant that requires a lot of it. The soil is porous, and most of the roots are gone, so you must water as often as the soil feels dry. In summer, especially as your bonsai grows older and is ready for an outdoor vacation, you may need to water daily.

Pruning is the other maintenance chore. Check your bonsai often to make sure it is growing into the composition you envisioned. Use wire and pruning to achieve the ideal shape.

Feed your bonsai all-purpose plant food at half strength. Begin by feeding every other month. If foliage dulls, feed more often.

Forcing Flowering Trees and Shrubs

The flowering trees and shrubs that grow outdoors, both cultivated and wild, are dormant during the winter months, not the least bit dead. They are waiting for the spring to waken them, and spring speaks in easily duplicated voices —warmth and light. If you supply these, the plants will waken at your call and not wait for spring.

Forsythia is one of the easiest of all flowering shrubs to force into bloom, and the way it blooms is typical of all the other trees and shrubs. Given light and warmth, and water of course, in a week to 10 days, the branches will put out their first sign of life: very small, sometimes pale, flowers. Forsythia, like many flowering trees and shrubs, blooms before it leafs out. After the blooms have gone by, and sometimes before they are over, small leaves will appear.

These will stay on the branches for a very long time—several weeks, if their indoor home is a little on the cool side and not too sunny.

Forsythia will do even more than flower or leaf. Occasionally, branches that I have forced into winter bloom have put out roots right in the vase water. Once I successfully transplanted my forced, rooted branches outdoors and ended up with a whole new forsythia bush.

Flowering Plants to Force

Those high-priced flowering branches offered by florists in late winter can be forced by you just as successfully as by the growers.

Some of those my friends and I force without difficulty are: apple, quince, flowering cherry, flowering crab, flowering plum, flowering peach (though I've found this harder, and the flowers less than striking) and forsythia. I envied a Vermont neighbor who achieved great results with lilac—tiny, tiny lilac flowers in pale colors would appear on her forced branches, along with the small delicate leaves. This list includes the flowering trees and shrubs found in most backyard gardens and on patios in containers, primarily in northern areas. But flowering trees and shrubs in warmer regions can also be forced. Where spring arrives earlier, however, forcing has less appeal since winter is almost over.

Wild plants can be forced, too. Pussy willow cut toward the end of winter, before there is any sign

---

For many, bonsai is a full-time hobby. Results are both the gardener's and decorator's joy— this planting is never ignored.

of swelling at the bud joints, will fuzz out when brought indoors to warmth and light. If there are no blooming trees or shrubs in your area, and you would like to see some young green leaves before the snows melt, cut and force young branch ends—almost any wildling is willing to put out a few leaves if conditions are right. It's rather fun to force into leaf a plant you don't recognize—then to try to guess what you've brought in.

As a rule of thumb, branches we force are cut with discretion from plants that can afford to give up a few branches. But it would be a waste to cut and force rhododendrons since most are evergreen and each bloom is so spectacular.

Cutting the Branches

The right time to cut branches for forcing is toward the end of winter. Although the flowers and leaf buds are set earlier, they aren't ready for forcing in the dead of winter. I cut mine on a warm day, and preferably one that follows one or two other warm days. If nature has done a little of the forcing, what remains to be done indoors usually goes faster.

When you approach the shrub or tree you plan to borrow a few early blooms from, think of the cutting you are about to do as pruning. With your eye, mark out the areas of the plant that are most heavily branched. Cut away any branches that seem to be growing in a direction that interferes with others or that may rub against others when the wind blows. Cut as many branches as will improve the spacing of other branches.

Although forced branches in bloom are really dazzling in large displays, they can also be cut down for small arrangements.

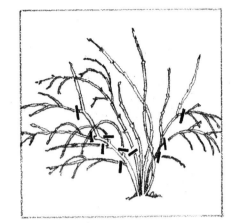

Cut flowering branches for forcing at the points indicated.

Not all the branches you pruned for the good of the plant will be thick with blossoms. Some plants flower on new wood; some flower on old wood. Branches that will have a lot of blooms have a lot of nodes from which buds will spring. Some show the beginnings of buds even in the dead of winter. Once you have cut away as many branches as will improve the shape and appearance of the plant, then cut a few heavily budded branches from the back of the plant to improve the bouquet.

Forcing the Branches

Put the branches either into snow in a big pot, or into water, and set them in a cool room for a day or so. Before I put mine into water, if the growth is thick and woody, I hammer them a little at the tough ends—for about 3 inches along the stem—to make it easier for the plant to take up water.

After the snow in the pot has melted, I move the branches to a

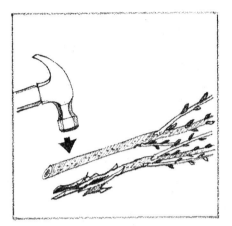

Crush branch ends to aid water absorption and to speed blooming.

table a few feet back from a sunny window in my coolest room. The blooms won't last in a hot room.

Care of Forced Branches

In order to keep the flowers alive as long as possible, change the water every day or so to keep it clean and fresh. When the flowers have come out, move the forced branches away from any direct sunlight. Then, at night, move the vase to the coolest place in the house, or open a nearby window. Make sure the open window doesn't blow a frosty draft on tender African violets and other tropical houseplants.

When the flowers begin to fade, don't rush to discard your forced branches, as they will usually produce a charming second crop of pale leaves. And, if you want to, let the leaves live as long as you can, just in case the branch you've cut is willing to root and provide you with a new plant for your outdoor garden.

FROM SEEDS: A HOUSE FULL OF PLANTS

You can hold enough seeds in the palm of your hand to fill your house from end to end with houseplants, from the adorable wax begonias to stately, ceiling-high scheffleras. About the only hazard in growing houseplants from seed is overplanting! Some of these seeds are free (see list). Commercial seeds range in price from 45 cents to $1.00 per packet and contain a minimum of 10 seeds, but usually many more. Starting 10 to 20 asparagus-ferns is, in my view, overplanting. So, when you buy houseplant seeds, make it a cooperative venture with gardening neighbors, or you'll find yourself in the garden supply business—trying to get rid of over-abundance!

The following lists catalog houseplants that can be grown from seed and houseplants for which seeds are generally available. Although finding seed for the species and variety you want to grow isn't always easy, that needn't stop you from trying to start new houseplants from scratch. Many of those that can be propagated by seed can be propagated in other ways as well (see page 58–71). And some seeds don't have to be purchased at all. Some of the herbs and spice seeds on your cupboard shelves make great houseplants (and fun projects for kids), as do many things you may once have considered kitchen discards, such as avocado pits and citrus seeds.

You'd think that seeds, which were designed to sprout in the open air under the sky, would balk at being housebound, but they don't. To sprout indoors, seeds need extra moisture and warmth, and both are usually easier to supply indoors than outdoors.

The equipment needed for starting seeds is minimal. You already have most of it. Containers, a rooting medium such as vermiculite or milled sphagnum moss or ground peat moss, the seeds and plastic to hold in moisture—these are the basics. Once the babies have grown, you will transplant them following directions beginning on page 73. Then you will need pots—and pots and pots. But that's about it. When you are involved with the growing plants from seeds, the investment is mainly one of time, patience and love.

Common Houseplants from Seed

These are current offerings in the popular garden catalogs—plants for which seeds are fairly easy to find.

African violet
  Saintpaulia
Alpine strawberry
  Fragaria
Asparagus-fern
  Asparagus sprengeri
Balsam
  Impatiens balsamina
Begonia, wax, fibrous-rooted
  Begonia
Browallia
  Browallia
Cactus
Calceolaria
  Calceolaria
Christmas cherry;
  Jerusalem cherry
  Solanum pseudo-capsicum
Christmas pepper
  Capsicum
Cineraria
  Senecio
Coleus
  Coleus
Cyclamen
  Cyclamen
Geranium
  Pelargonium
Gerbera
  Gerbera
Gloxinia
  Sinningia
Impatiens
  Impatiens
Lantana
  Lantana
Mimosa
  Mimosa
Persian violet; exacum
  Exacum
Petunia
  Petunia
Primrose
  Primula polyantha

Other Houseplants from Seed

These are not currently offered in my catalogs. Some seeds can be found in your kitchen, for instance, avocado and citrus; others, like Jerusalem or Christmas cherry, can be gathered from your own or friends' houseplants. There are also specialized catalogs that offer the more exotic seeds. If seeds for a plant you particularly want seem impossible to find, check pages 60–61 and 67 to see if they can be grown from cuttings and

Start from seed; take your sunniest window; mix and match your plantings; use your imagination to create a never-ending greenhouse corner.

Seeds can be started indoors in almost any kind of container that is at least 3 inches deep. Popular containers include: peat pots (left); clay pots (middle); flats (right).

pages 64–65 for the possibility of root division.

Avocado (pit)
  Persea
Bishop's cap
  Astrophytum
Cape primrose
  Streptocarpus
Chinese evergreen
  Aglaonema
Citrus (pit)
Coffee tree
  Coffea
Coral berry
  Ardisia
Living stones; stone-face
  Lithops
Mexican foxglove
  Allophyton
Norfolk Island pine
  Araucaria heterophylla
Ponytail; bottle palm
  Beaucarnea

Rosary vine
  Ceropegia woodii
Rose, miniature
  Rosa
Rouge berry; bloodberry
  Rivina
Schefflera
  Brassaia

Equipment for Starting Seeds

For growing plants from seeds indoors, the first thing you must do is find the right containers to sprout seeds in. The popular methods for starting seeds indoors, and some pots and flats used, are shown above. Flats are rectangular boxes made of wood, pressed peat or pressed cardboard, sold by garden supply centers—or saved from seedlings purchased at the local greenhouse.

However, you can improvise many containers suitable for starting seedlings. Quart-size milk cartons, cut in half lengthwise, are just about the right depth. Quart-size jars and larger ones will work, too. So will plastic containers, such as those used for cottage cheese. You can use big tin cans, loaf pans, old refrigerator trays—almost anything that will hold planting material and is at least 3 inches deep.

Planting is done in a combination of potting soil and commercial products such as sphagnum moss or ground peat moss and vermiculite. Both hold moisture well and are sterile. Fill the bottom of the container to within 1½ inches of the top with potting soil; top it with ½ inch of either sphagnum moss or vermiculite.

The seedlings start and sprout in the loose, sterile material, and as the roots grow downward, they reach into soil rich in nutrients. This extra-rich soil makes strong seedlings.

In addition to planting mediums and containers, you will need clear plastic (cleaners' bags, for instance) to tent these miniature plant beds after sowing is completed, saucers for draining containers and labels. You may think you'll remember what was planted where, but you won't. Labels serve another purpose: They make good stakes to hold up the plastic tents, as shown below.

Growing Your Own Bright Begonias

I love wax begonias because of the cheerful red, pink or white blooms which are borne in masses in spring and summer and, in my experience, more sparsely the rest of the year. The reddish-leaf types with red or coral blossoms are an

Tenting keeps moisture and temperature even. Use the label as a pole.

attractive contrast to the green of most indoor plants. Wax begonias (pictured on page 63) are easy to start from seeds. They require about three months to grow into seedlings of the size you buy for setting out in spring.

The way begonia seeds are sown is typical of the sowing of most houseplant seeds. Unless you are going to grow some in late winter or early spring for setting out as well as for indoor use, you won't want to plant a whole packet of seed. A dozen begonias should be enough. You can sow one seed in each of a dozen 3-inch pots and not have to transplant the seedlings for some time. But they are easier to care for if you sow a dozen seeds to a flat or, following the pot-in-pot method shown at left, in the space between two pots. A dozen pots covered with plastic tenting occupying your favorite windowsills aren't attractive. Planted in a single flat, they will occupy only one spot, and all the seedlings will be cared for at once. Also, soil in tiny pots tends to dry out almost in hours when the heat is on, so you lose seedlings easily, or spend a lot of time making sure each and every one is evenly moist.

After you have selected the container, fill it with regular potting soil to within ½ to 1 inch of the top. Add ½ inch of milled sphagnum moss or vermiculite. Gently firm and level this planting bed, then sow the seeds in rows 2 inches apart. Seeds planted too close together prevent good air circulation and encourage the one real enemy of seedlings—a fungus called "damping-off." Usually it is the result of poor air circulation and moist soil. Damping-off fungus grows from organisms in the soil, and that is one reason to start seedlings in pasteurized commer-

A hole in the tents helps plants acclimatize to house conditions.

cial potting soil and sterile moss or vermiculite, rather than in soil from the outdoor garden.

The finest seeds (some look almost like dust) do not need to be covered with soil after sowing. Just scatter these over the planting medium. Cover larger seeds the depth of their own diameter. Label each planting, giving the sowing date, the species and variety; for instance, Begonia, 'Vodka.' Place the container in lukewarm water to absorb moisture. When beads of water appear on the surface soil, remove the container and let it drain, then drape plastic over the labels and secure the folds loosely at the bottom.

Place the seedlings in good light in a warm room. Temperatures between 72 and 80 degrees help speed germination. Check the seedlings daily. Never let the soil dry out. Water from the bottom, if practical, or water the top very gently when the surface soil shows signs of drying. Soil should be evenly moist but never soggy wet.

As soon as the seeds show signs of germination, place the

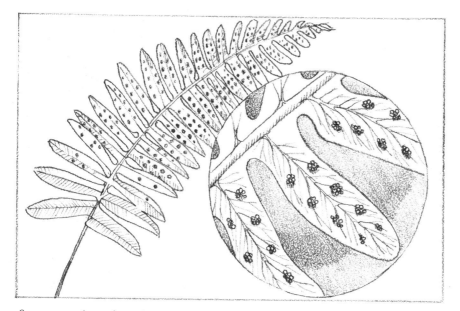

Spores are found on the underside of fern fronds. When the spore cases begin to open, it's time to start collecting.

containers in bright light. Make an effort to provide fresh air daily, but don't let cold drafts flow over the containers. Open the tenting for a few hours daily. As the seedlings begin to grow you can provide more fresh air by poking holes in the tenting. By the time the seedlings are two weeks old, they should have had sufficient exposure to room air to be ready to come out of their tenting. At this point, begonia seedlings can be transplanted and moved to a permanent home in a sunny east or west window. Transplant the seedlings (see page 73). Use African-violet soil. As soon as growth begins, fertilize plants regularly every two weeks with half strength solutions of 5-10-5 food for blooming plants.

This type of begonia is also propagated by tip cuttings (see pages 58–64).

Care of Wax Begonias
Wax begonias prefer temperatures between 60 and 70 degrees and do best when soil is kept evenly moist. Water only when the soil begins to feel a little damp. Pinch back tips of young plants to keep growth compact and shapely.

Propagating Ferns
Have you ever seen a fern frond patterned with brown speckles on the underside? When I was a child, I thought the brown flecks were insects. But they are fern spores, the equivalent of seeds.

We may think that all vegetation starts from seed but this isn't so. Plants have many other ways of reproducing. Ferns are among the most primitive plants on the planet. They date all the way back to a time when the world was watery, and so it isn't surprising that their way of reproducing is different.

You can find fern spores in the woods in summer and early fall. In my area, maidenhair and Boston ferns grow wild, and these are among the ferns that make good houseplants. You can also buy fern spores from catalogs. The asparagus-fern is also offered by many, but remember that this

lovely plant is an asparagus, not a fern.

If you want to start from scratch comb the woods in late summer for specimens with the brown flecking of spore patterns. The spores are in cases (see illustration left). When these are partially open, turn the fronds upside down and shake them hard into a clean brown paper bag. You can also cut the fronds into pieces.

Whether you are planting spores acquired from a seedman or specimens captured from the wild, the planting procedure is similar. A good container for this type of propagation is a bulb pan (see page 48), which provides some depth of soil to hold moisture. Terrarium potting soil or regular all-purpose potting soil mixed well with ¼ part humus is a good growing medium.

If you are planting loose spores, sprinkle them over the surface of well-moistened soil. Do not press them into the soil and don't cover them with more soil. If you are planting pieces of cut-up, fern-bearing spores, set them as illustrated, spore side down, on the soil surface. Slide a plastic bag over the container and seal it loosely with a twist tie. Set the container in a warm room, between 65 and 75 degrees, in a spot where the light is good, but not in direct sunlight. Keep soil damp.

The next step is to be *very* patient. Growth may appear in a few weeks, and it could also take a year, depending on the kind of fern and the age of the spores. The first growth will be a mosslike greening of the soil. When this shows solid, gently break it up into small pieces and set each piece on a surface of moist sand and peat moss mixed half and half. Put a plastic tent over this planting and set the container in a warm, bright spot. Fern fronds will grow from the moss.

When they are growing sturdily, transplant the ferns to African-violet soil or terrarium soil (see page 73).

Care of Indoor Ferns

The best light for most indoor ferns is near a sunny east or west window. A south window will also work if there are other plants between the ferns and window to cut the direct sun. Tiny ferns thrive in fluorescent gardens. Temperatures of between 60 and 70 degrees are suitable, but the key to success is moist, fresh air. Ferns turn brown in hot, stale air. Daily misting does wonders. You must water enough to keep the soil evenly moist. Feed an all-purpose plant food following container directions.

Food Plants from Scratch

I class tomatoes, cucumbers, squash, melons and eggplants as economical houseplants because starting them from seed in the house really saves cash. For a fraction of what it costs to buy grown seedlings to set out when the weather warms, you can start dozens of seeds on their way to becoming seedlings six to eight weeks before it is time to plant the outdoor garden.

Cherry and patio-type tomatoes are really inexpensive houseplants since they can be grown from seed and thrive indoors, if you have six hours of direct sun daily. I start cucumbers and squash indoors to get a jump on the season, and I have crops ready for picking weeks before crops grown from seed planted outdoors will be ready. I start melons and eggplants indoors

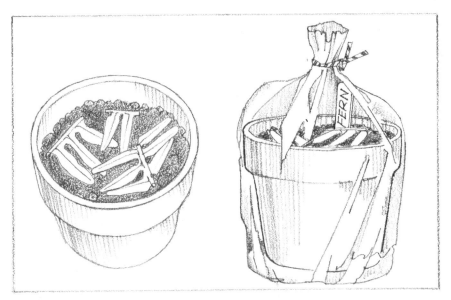

Place cut-up fern frond pieces face down on soil. Tenting the pot keeps moisture in and speeds germination.

because in the areas where I have gardened, the season isn't long enough to ripen these luxuries if they are started from seed sown outdoors.

Growing Tomatoes Indoors

The way that tomatoes are started indoors and transplanted can serve as a guide to the handling of other food plants you might want to start early indoors. You can start seeds for tomatoes for the garden at the same time you start your tomatoes to be cultivated as houseplants. Be careful in your choice of variety. Only the tiny tomato varieties can be ripened indoors—the big tomatoes require too much room and more light than you can provide. Tiny Tim and Pixie Hybrid are good examples of tomatoes suitable for indoors.

Containers and soils for starting food plants indoors are the same as those used for starting houseplants from seed (see page 32). To grow tiny tomatoes indoors, you might start the seeds in a flat (see page 32), then transfer them to a hanging basket, a home that shows them off and suits them particularly well.

You may have some hanging basket containers left over from last summer, or you can buy them at garden supply centers. But if you want to save money, you'll make your own. Any rigid plastic container that will hold two quarts of soil will do; for instance, a one-gallon plastic milk container with the top cut off.

To create good drainage, heat a knitting needle and poke four tiny holes through the bottom of the plastic container. Then poke three larger holes around the sides at the top so you can attach the hanger cords for hanging the basket. Tie a discarded aluminum pie plate underneath to catch the drips from watering. To make the hangers, use three pieces of strong cord, knotted into the side holes and tied together at the top. You can also use wire coat hangers to make hanging wires similar to those found on purchased hanging baskets.

The potting mix I am about to suggest is the one used by the USDA's Marc Cathey, who has investigated the growing of tomatoes in hanging baskets. The basic mix is equal parts of peat moss and vermiculite. Fertilize each half bushel of potting mix (that's 16 quarts, or enough for 8 hanging baskets) by adding ¼ cup of pulverized dolomitic limestone, ¼ cup of 20-percent superphosphate and ⅛ cup of a 5-10-5 fertilizer. The mixture may be stored, once prepared, for future use. If you are going to try only a few baskets and don't have supplies of limestone or superphosphate, add a 5-10-5 fertilizer for blooming houseplants instead. Fill your baskets to within 2 inches of the top, leaving enough room for convenient watering.

Sow your tomato seeds in flats as instructed for begonia seeds (see page 33). Thin seedlings as they become crowded in the flat. I plant three seeds for every seedling I require, so I can discard the two weakest.

When the seedlings are several inches tall, transplant to their hanging baskets, one to a basket. To transplant, scoop a hole in the basket soil deep enough to hold the seedling root ball so that the crown (top) of the root ball will be 1 inch below the basket rim. Set the roots in the soil, firming the soil around so that it holds the plant securely upright. Add more potting mixture, if necessary, to bring the soil level to 1 inch below the container rim. Water gently with lukewarm water, until the water drains out the bottom.

The next step is to hang the basket where it will receive at least six hours of direct sun daily. After two days, water again with a solution containing 1/5 the fertilizer recommended for flowering houseplants. Pick off any damaged or yellowing leaves. Turn the plant often so each side gets enough light. Prune branches that rub against each other.

Care of Tomatoes Indoors
If your tomato basket is kept well fed, evenly moist and in good light, it will show flowers and produce fruit within a month or two. The one enemy is white fly. To avoid it, make sure the room is aired daily and mist the plant at least once a day. Also, frequent showers help.

The Indoor Herb Garden

Many of the herbs that grow outdoors can be brought indoors in fall, and they will thrive all winter in a sunny window garden or in a fluorescent-light garden (see pages 8–13). Many others can be started from seed and grown from beginning to end as indoor plants. Included in this group are basil, sweet bay, chives, coriander, scented-leaf geraniums, oregano, parsley, rosemary, sage, southernwood, tarragon, thyme and lemon-verbena. I've had my best luck with parsley, sweet bay, basil, sage and chives.

Many of the herbs are slow starters. That is perhaps because many of them originated in such desertlike terrain that the plants evolved seeds that could sit for months, even years, in the ground without sprouting and remain in good condition.

The herbs that grow indoors produce less dense foliage than those growing outdoors, and require as much direct sunlight as you can give them. Many of them do very well in fluorescent-light gardens. A shelf full of herbs growing under lights in a corner of the kitchen makes a delightful display. If the kitchen is aired frequently and is on the cool side, the herbs will do even better—somewhere between 50 and 70 degrees is good. The moisture most kitchens generate helps to keep plants flourishing. I place my herbs on a tray filled with small pebbles and keep the tray half full of water at all times. The water level should be just below the pot bottoms, but not touching them.

All you need to make your own fluorescent garden is a source of electricity, a fluorescent fixture and fluorescent bulbs. A 48-inch industrial fixture that houses two 40-watt bulbs, one Gro-Lux and one Gro-Lux Wide Spectrum, is recommended for herbs. This size is large enough to light 36 three-inch pots or 20 four-inch pots.

Lights for herbs should be about 5 inches above the tops of the foliage and should be turned on for about 14 hours a day. If your plants become spindly, increase the light to 16 to 18 hours a day.

If you are growing your herbs on a windowsill, then treat them as you would begonias (see page 33). All-purpose potting soils are suitable for herbs. If you want to make a mix of your own, combine equal parts of garden loam, sand and fine-milled peat moss. If you are growing a whole collection of herbs in small pots, check them often, since the smaller pots dry out very quickly. Keep the tips of herbs pinched back. This encourages branching and makes prettier, more productive plants. It also provides you with flavorings for cooking. From January on, as days

---

For dramatic decorating impact as well as luscious harvest, plant baskets with one of the small variety tomatoes.

begin to lengthen, feed your houseplant herbs with a liquid plant food every two or three weeks. Choose a plant food for foliage plants.

Before selecting seeds to start indoors, check the hints and tips in the following list. Sow seeds in flats and handle as described for begonias (see page 33).

Basil: Sweet basil of the green-leaf type is best. It will grow on a sunny east, west or south windowsill or under lights. Keep tips pinched back. Mist and shower often to avoid white fly. This is an annual, so plant again next year.

Bay, sweet: Better to buy a started plant (see page 11) or beg a cutting from a friend, since germination of seeds is extremely slow.

Chives: Good in a sunny east, west or south window or under lights. Keep soil on the moist side, and mist often. Keep chive tops cut to keep the plant producing.

Dill: You can start and grow dill indoors under lights. Do not transplant. Start it in the pot that will be its home and keep it there. Keep tops pinched to make the plant grow compactly. An annual, so plan to replant next year.

Geranium, scented-leaf: A great houseplant. Grows in conditions suited to other geraniums (see page 11). Requires lots of direct sunlight or fluorescent light. Keep soil moist but not soggy. Mist often.

Marjoram, sweet: Start from seed indoors (it needs 10 to 15 days to sprout). Grow it outdoors in summer, then bring indoors in the fall (see page 11).

Double duty for fluorescents. Give a dark corner a lift by growing herbs under lights. The herbs will do better and so will the corner.

Oregano: Most plants sold as oregano are sweet marjoram—and the flower is similar. If you are a purist, look for seeds for *Origanum vulgare*, genuine oregano. Oregano will grow on a sunny windowsill or under lights. Keep the tops pinched back or the plant will get out of hand in size. It grows very quickly and is on the tall side.

Parsley: This is very slow to germinate but grows well once started. Plant several seeds to make a big potful, as indoor plants are spindlier than outdoor specimens. Grows well on a sunny east, west or south windowsill or under fluorescent lights. Plants growing outdoors can be potted up and brought indoors in fall. They'll fade by late winter, so in December start seeds to have plants ready to supply your late winter needs. In spring, you can set these plants outdoors for the summer.

Rosemary: Start as seed and be patient. Rosemary is slow to germinate. It makes a good houseplant if it can be kept on the cool side. The most successful rosemary I've ever met was set about 1 foot under and 3 feet back from a sunny south window in a New York apartment. Don't let rosemary dry out. It drinks water very quickly, so check it often. You can also bring in outdoor rosemary plants (see page 13).

Sage: Sage requires at least 14 days to germinate indoors and is much slower to sprout outdoors. It can be grown indoors under fluorescent lights, but it must be kept pinched back severely, since sage is a straggly plant and will quickly grow out of bounds.

Savory: Summer savory germinates in about a week or so, while winter savory (which is a perennial) takes much longer. The perennial

Weedy growth weakens plants.

To strengthen plants, clip leaves.

makes the better houseplant and succeeds under fluorescent lights.

Southernwood: This is a fragrance herb, not one used for flavoring. It is a big plant and, if frequently pruned back, makes a good houseplant. It will grow on a sill that has many hours of direct sunlight or under fluorescent lights.

Thyme: Thyme will grow from seed, but it takes 10 or more days to germinate indoors and three weeks or more outdoors. I've grown it indoors on a sunny west windowsill, though generally it needs a lot of sun. The leaves are very tiny, but they are flavorful. You can bring thyme in from outdoors (see page 13).

Verbena, lemon: This can be handled as a houseplant under fluorescent lights, but it is best to buy started plants (see page 13).

Cupboard Seeds and Kitchen Discards

Any time that you look at your houseplants and wonder how you are going to keep the plants alive, turn to this page for reassurance. Plants have an extraordinarily strong impulse to live. Nothing can prove it to you more clearly than the astonishing variety of things that will grow from seeds found in your kitchen cupboard and even kitchen discards.

For instance, a friend planted a grapefruit seed—not from a fresh grapefruit, but a seed she found in a can of processed grapefruit. And today that seed has become a large, handsome houseplant! Don't ask me how—I don't know. When I was writing a book on Oriental cooking, I planted a coriander seed on a hunch. It grew— as I suspected it would—into the green herb we call Chinese parsley. Those coriander seeds had been on my shelf for a couple of years. Surely before that, they had sat on the grocer's shelf and in the herb grower's drying room.

If you do not find it extraordinary that old and canned seeds are able to grow plants, take a minute to be amazed at how plant parts will evolve into new plants. Beginning on page 58 there are instructions for developing

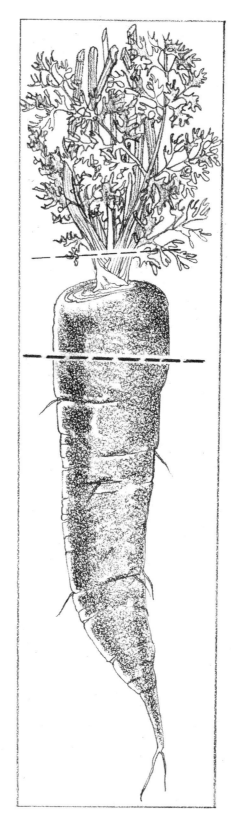

Broken lines indicate where to cut carrot; then remove the ferns.

new plants by rooting leaf and tip cuttings. These are common propagation (reproductive) methods. But the carrot is even more amazing. It will grow leaves from a cut-off top, and, surprisingly, so will the pineapple.

The projects described on the following pages may not make the most glamorous houseplants you've ever seen (though an avocado tree certainly rivals many expensive indoor plants in interest and beauty), but they are fun, and they will fascinate children.

Growing Carrot Plants

I suspect that carrots are among the most eager to grow of all nature's creations. The carrot's prime interest seems to be in producing its green, fernlike top. That's logical, since its seeds are produced from the flowers that develop among the greenery.

There are several ways to go about making a cut carrot regrow its greenery. The first method results in a tiny forest that will grow in a shallow glass dish. Choose plump carrots that have fresh, unwilted green tops and shiny skin. Older carrots have yellow, wilted greenery, which growers usually cut off since it makes the product look unappetizing. Older carrots have a wizened look to the skin. Very fresh carrots look "plump."

Cut away the top half inch of the carrot, just below the area from which the green ferns are growing. Remove the fern tops as illustrated. What remains is a stub of a carrot top. Set this in a shallow bowl filled with lukewarm fresh water. The water should reach about halfway up the sides of the carrot top. Don't let the water dry up. In a few days, you should see signs of growth among the stubs of the carrot ferns, and

Cut-off carrot top is set in dish with water to sprout new greenery.

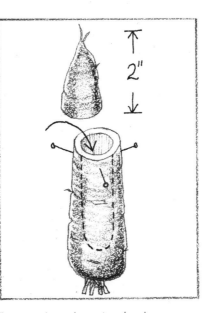

For a unique hanging basket, cut. carrot as shown and fill with water.

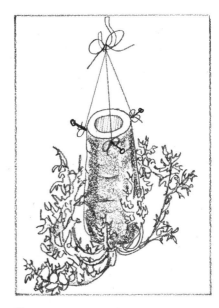

Carrot soon sprouts new greens which grow upward and cover it.

soon a miniature forest of ferny carrot leaves will develop.

The second method for making carrots into mini-houseplants is more complicated—but more fun. It is important that you begin with a very fresh carrot. Cut away the bottom tip, 2 to 3 inches on the average carrot, and all of the greenery, leaving ½ inch of stub. Next, drive a slender nail into the carrot's cut bottom end about ½ inch from the cut. Remove the nail and repeat the step in two other places on opposite sides of the carrot level with the first spot. You are creating holes from which to suspend the carrot. Now, working at the same end of the carrot, with a sharp knife or apple corer, hollow out the carrot to a depth of 1 to 2 inches.

Next, with strong string or thin florist's wire, make a three-strand suspension hanger for the carrot, similar to those used to suspend hanging baskets. Fill the center of the hollowed-out carrot with water and hang the carrot in a sunny window. Keep the hollow end filled with water, and leaves will begin to grow from the other end. The plant will eventually become a charming little hanging basket surrounding itself with its own greenery. A group of hanging carrot baskets is even more fun.

Growing a Pineapple Plant

The next time you have a fresh pineapple at your house, don't discard the top. You can grow it into a charming pineapple plant— attractive enough to use as a centerpiece.

The first step is to slice off the pineapple top about ½ inch below the base of the foliage. Set the top to dry on a well-lighted windowsill for about 24 hours. Next, fill a cereal bowl with clean sand (not sea sand) and set the pineapple, cut end down, on the sand. Add enough water to moisten the sand thoroughly and keep the sand moist. Return the pineapple to a sunny windowsill, and in six to eight weeks, the cut end should begin to form roots.

The plant is now ready for potting. Choose a container large enough to hold the pineapple top comfortably, fill it with 2 to 3 inches of pebbles to improve drainage, then add enough potting soil (all-purpose will do) to bring the crown of the pineapple top to within 2 inches of the pot rim. Lift the pineapple gently from its sand base onto the soil, then fill the pot with soil to the top of the crown and firm the soil. Water well. Cover the top of the pot with a clear plastic bag, gathered loosely at the base of the pot. Water weekly or when the soil begins to dry. Feed the plant with a plant food for blooming plants every two weeks in spring and summer, monthly in fall and winter. In about two years, the plant should begin to grow a fruit, a real pineapple! This develops upward on a long stem, which grows from the foliage cluster.

Growing an Avocado Tree

You can grow very beautiful houseplants from avocado pits and the seeds from all kinds of citrus fruits. The big seed at the heart of an avocado will sprout a stem that in time becomes a ceiling-high tree. The best-looking one I ever saw spread over half of a large country living room. Growing outdoors in the warm climates to which it is native, the avocado becomes a big tree. Indoors, it will go up to the ceiling and then will spread its branches outward. Its shape is controlled by your pruning. The oldest one I ever had was five years old and so big I couldn't take it with me when I moved.

The best-known method for starting an avocado is to root the pit in water. The first step is to rinse the pit in clean water. Then, about halfway between the pointed top and the broad base, poke three toothpicks into the pit at equal distances from each other. Place the pit, broad base down, into a jar or glass filled with water. The toothpicks will keep the pit from sinking into the jar. Keep the water level constant around the base of the pit. You can set the jar in a dark place, as some gardeners recommend, but I like to keep mine on a kitchen sill where there is sun—otherwise I tend to forget to keep the water level constant. In a few weeks, generally, the pit cracks, and roots grow from the base, while a slender reddish-green shoot grows from the tip.

Should you happen to let the water dry out after the seed has started to root, don't throw it out. That once happened to me. I filled the glass with water, and the pit rooted again. It produced not one but three handsome shoots that became the best-looking avocado plant I've ever grown.

One of the problems with avocados is that single shoot that goes straight up. The first one I ever tried went straight up about 4 feet before it developed any leaves,

and what I finally had as a houseplant was a 6-foot stalk with a few leaves at the top. Not very ornamental. By the time an avocado is that tall it is rather difficult to prune it into a graceful plant. But there are ways to avoid the beanstalk trip it likes to take.

Gardeners who root avocados in dark places generally move them to the light when the leaves begin to show—but not into direct sunlight. They let it grow to 8 inches tall, then cut it back (be ruthless!) to half its height. When it has soared again to 8 inches, pot it in moist soil, leaving the top third of the pit exposed.

I plant avocados below the soil surface after their roots have sprouted. I start a set of four in an 11-inch pot which has several inches of gravel in the bottom for drainage and is filled with all-purpose soil. I plant four because it makes a thicker plant at once. As the plants begin to crowd each other seriously, I remove the two weakest, leaving the two stalwart plants to fill the pot. I prune the sprouts back by half as soon as they get to be 8 inches tall, hoping the plant will form a new main stem. I keep pruning the tips after each 12 inches or so of growth. This makes the tree branch frequently and, in the end, you have a many-branched, many-leaved plant that will go right to the ceiling. Since indoor trees are expensive to buy, and the avocado is free, it is worth spending some effort to make it beautiful.

Care of an Avocado Tree
Indoors, the avocado is evergreen, but it shows less growth in winter. In dry, airless rooms, it is attacked by red spider-mite—an almost invisible little thing that shows up as tiny yellow spots on the leaves. To avoid red spider-mite,

air the room often, and mist the plant daily if you can. There are some indoor sprays that help control red spider-mite, but I use sprays only as a last resort. When the plant is young, you should shower it monthly. It perks up the avocado and helps keep spider-mites away.

Avocados need good light, but I find they burn in direct sunlight. I've had most success with mine when they were just to the left or right of a bright east or west window or, if there is lots of sun in the winter, in a north window. In the summer, if you can, place the plant outdoors in a light but not sunny corner. The fresh air and moisture outdoors makes a strong, healthy plant better able to stand up to hot, dry winters indoors. Temperatures over 75 degrees cause the avocado to suffer and leave it prey to red spider-mite.

Keep the avocado soil evenly moist. If it dries enough so that the leaves wilt, they'll brown around the edges. If this happens, water the plant well and mist the leaves at once to help them recover quickly.

Feed your avocados all-purpose foliage plant food all year 'round, about every second watering.

Cultivating the Evergreen Citrus
That pretty citrus shrub with tiny oranges that you find in florist's shops is no prettier than the citrus shrubs you can grow from seeds taken from the citrus fruit you eat in your home. Seeds of any of the following citrus fruit can be sown: lemons, limes, oranges, grapefruit. The only ones I haven't tried are

---

Kitchen discards can produce some terrific houseplants; orange and lemon trees are not unusual. Add a Jerusalem cherry for more color.

tangerines. Although the leaves differ a little, the overall effect is the same with any of the citrus—a dark green evergreen leaf on a compactly growing, sturdy plant that is fairly easy to maintain.

The one caution I offer is that they are slow to grow—you won't have an overnight shrub. You aren't likely to have an overnight sprout either, since the citrus seeds take a while to develop shoots.

First step is to wash the seeds and let them dry overnight on a windowsill. Then, plant 20 or more in a shallow flat (see page 32). Space seeds 1 inch apart. Cover the seeds with a light sprinkling of vermiculite (about ¾ inch). Keep the flat moist in a warm, sunny spot until the leaves have developed. Turn the flat often so all sides receive an equal amount of light. Without equal light, you'll find the seedlings bending toward the light and growing crooked.

By the time a second pair of leaves appears on the seedlings, the flat will start to get crowded. Gently remove the weakest seedlings. In a few more weeks, the remaining seedlings again will be crowding the pot. Discard the weakest once more, leaving about a dozen seedlings.

Now transplant the seedlings (see page 73). Plant them in African-violet soil, and after a few days' rest in semilight, set them in your sunniest window, east, west or south. Keep the soil evenly moist, but let the soil dry out a little between waterings. Citrus plants hate being either very wet or very dry. If the soil really dries out, most of the leaves will fall off, and the plants may die.

Care of Citrus Plants

The citruses will go on year after year, slowly reaching shrub size,

Thin out your citrus seedlings, once they have taken hold, so they will develop into a potful of handsome greens.

always green and shiny—very handsome, indeed. They may produce fragrant, small white blossoms, and some will even give fruit. I once came across a tree-size lemon plant that grew indoors in the northwest corner of Connecticut, where winters are cold and the light not all that great. It was summered outdoors, and that is the secret to success with the citruses. They respond beautifully, and grow much more quickly, if set in the shelter of a tall shrub or small tree in a spot where they receive an hour or two of direct sun each day.

The best temperature range for the citruses are in rooms where temperatures stay between 60 and 70 degrees. Air the room daily, and mist to give the atmosphere a little humidity.

Feed your citrus plants blooming-type plant food all year, following container directions. Should the leaves begin to show a yellow speckling, feed with an

acid-type plant food or diluted chelated iron.

As the original container becomes crowded, transplant smaller plants to another container, leaving a lot of room for the remaining plants to branch out. They'll go straight up in the air with few leaves along the bottom stems if overcrowded.

Growing a Sweet Potato Vine

Would you like a vine climbing the kitchen window? You can grow one for the cost of a fresh sweet potato.

The sweet potato is a tuber related to the morning glory, whose blue, pink or white trumpets grace so many American porches in summer. Rooting a sweet potato is rather like rooting an avocado (see pages 41–42). Stick 3 toothpicks into the middle of the tuber, and set the tapered end into a glass of water so that the bottom inch is covered. Set the glass in a brightly lighted window but not in

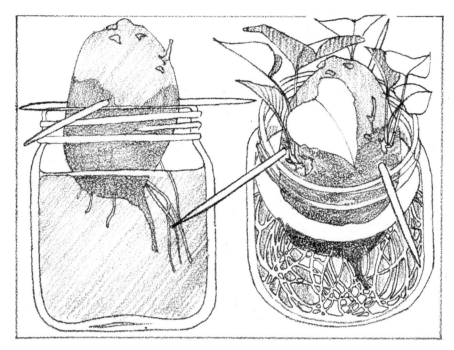

Suspend a sweet potato tuber in a glass of water just as you would an avocado pit; when the bottom is thick with roots, transplant.

direct sunlight. In a couple of weeks, the bottom end will show roots, and when this has become a thick mat of roots, it is time to transplant. Be sure to keep the water level even during the rooting period.

To transplant the sweet potato, select a pot or container at least 6 inches across. Fill the bottom with 2 to 3 inches of small pebbles for good drainage, then add blooming-type potting soil, enough to bring the top of the tuber to about 2 inches below the pot rim. Set the tuber on its side, at a slight angle, roots downward. Cover with soil to the top. Make a slight depression in the soil around the pot edges to catch and hold water or the water will run off.

Care of a Sweet Potato Vine

Set the plant in partial sun, not direct sunlight. My preferred place is on a ledge just a little below a brightly lighted kitchen window. Keep the soil moist but never soggy wet. Feed blooming-type plant food every two or three weeks. In a month or so, there should be one or two dozen sprouts, each with many leaves growing tendril fashion. Fasten thick, soft cord to the window frame and train the tendrils up the cord.

A different way to handle a sweet potato plant is to keep the branches cut to force leafing. It will grow into a lush, low houseplant in time.

Growing a Ginger Jar

Another fun project, and practical if you use ginger in your house, is to grow gingerroot. Buy fresh gingerroot at a Chinese specialty shop and bury it just below the surface in moist all-purpose potting soil. Set it in a closet to sprout, then in a sunny window and watch it grow tall pointed greenery. Kept evenly moist, the greenery and the root will develop and grow. In time, you will have a potful of fresh ginger to cook with and from which to start new pots of ginger growing.

Growing a Bean Pot

A bean pot is another popular kitchen discard project. Scatter a handful of dried beans over a potful of moist soil and watch them sprout almost overnight. They'll reach for the sky almost at once, especially if the pot is placed below the light source. They won't last long because the sprouts become weak as they grow tall, but children enjoy watching them grow. And you can add the sprouts to a salad.

Almost any of the seeds in your herb and spice rack are worth trying in soil. I mentioned before that I had successfully sprouted coriander, dill, caraway, fennel and mustard seeds—the list is as big as your spice and herb shelf.

FROM FORCED BULBS: MIDWINTER BLOSSOM

Have you ever pressed your nose to a florist's window somewhere between January and March, and wished you could afford to fill your house with pots and pots of bulbs in bloom—tulips, daffodils, fragrant narcissus and hyacinths— during the winter months? Well, you can if you buy the bulbs in the ready-to-plant stage instead of in the blooming stage.

Most of the spring-flowering bulbs can be brought into bloom indoors several months before they will flower outdoors, and there is no great expenditure involved. Consider your decorating schemes before you buy your bulbs, and plan how and where you will use each potful. Buy extra bulbs for gifts.

Forcing is a simple process that leads plants to believe they've been in the cold ground for months, that winter is over, and it's time to bloom. What actually happens is that they are planted in pots, chilled outdoors or in a cold cellar, garage or attic. Then they are brought into the artificial warmth of the indoors. I'll have to qualify that statement: This kind of forcing applies to spring bulbs. Amaryllis is forced into bloom simply by planting and watering.

Variety in size and color makes decorating with flowering bulbs an exciting yet remarkably easy job. For continued bloom, pot both early and late varieties.

For good indoor bloom of the spring bulbs, buy bulbs of the size described as "exhibition" or "first size." Garden supply centers also offer bulbs labeled "pre-chilled" or "for forcing." These are pre-chilled for several weeks by the distributors. The chilling period you put them through, about 12 or 13 weeks, can be shortened by the number of weeks of chilling already allowed. To learn exactly how many weeks of chilling the bulbs have had, ask the distributor. Generally, it's three to four weeks.

The Most Popular Bulbs

Since bulbs, like flowers, come in many varieties, you can choose a variety whose individual blooming schedule fits your timetable. Some varieties bloom "early," that is, in the late winter; others bloom in spring. For January or February forcing, choose "early" varieties; for March or April forcing, choose "late" varieties. Here are some of the best varieties for forcing, recommended by the Department of Agriculture and by the Netherlands Flower-bulb Institute.

EARLY TULIPS
(Bloom January, February)

Red:
  Bing Crosby
  Cassini
  Charles
  Christmas Marvel
  Olaf
  Paul Richter
  Prominence
  Topscore
  Trance
Yellow:
  Bellona
  Lavent

White:
  Pax
  Snow Star
Salmon:
  Apricot Beauty
Pink:
  Preludium
Variegated:
  Madame Spoor
  Merry Widow
  Roland

LATE TULIPS
(Bloom March, April)

Red:
  Couleur Cardinal
  Red Queen
  Robinea
  Utopia
Yellow:
  Makassar
  Ornament
White:
  Blizzard
Orange:
  Orange Sun
Pink:
  Peerless Pink
  Pink Supreme
  Rose Beauty
Variegated:
  Carl M. Bellman
  Edith Eddy
  Golden Eddy
  Paris
  United Europe

EARLY HYACINTHS
(Bloom January, February)

Red:
  Jan Bos
Pink:
  Anna Marie
  Eros
  Lady Derby
Blue:
  Bismarck
  Ostara
White:
  Carnegie
  L'Innocence

LATE HYACINTHS
(Bloom March, April)

Pink:
   Lady Derby
   Marconi
   Pink Pearl
Blue:
   Ostara
   Blue Giant
   Perle Brilliante
White:
   Carnegie

EARLY DAFFODILS
(Bloom January, February)

   Carlton
   Golden Harvest
   King Alfred

LATE DAFFODILS
(Bloom March, April)

   Cheerfulness
   Geranium
   Gold Medal
   Rembrandt
   Van Sion

CROCUS
(Bloom January, February)

   Grand Maitre
   Joan of Arc
   Peter Pan
   Pickwick
   Remembrance

The paper-white narcissus, often called just "paper-white," has been omitted from this list because its popularity puts it in a class by itself. Narcissus is the genus to which the daffodil belongs. The paper-whites have tall, slender leaves and white flowers on slim, elegant stems. Their fragrance is exquisite. They will perfume a whole room for days. Paper-whites can be forced for Thanksgiving or later, and they are sold everywhere plant materials are offered. Buy good quality bulbs —you'll get more blooms per bulb.

Containers for Forcing Bulbs

The container you choose will depend on the bulb size, on whether you plan to force the bulbs in pebbles and water or in soil, and on whether you plan to chill the bulbs outdoors or in a cool indoor spot. The growing medium (pebbles and water, or soil) for forced bulbs is needed to keep the bulb supplied with moisture and to keep it upright. It is not intended to feed the bulb, for the bulb already has all the nutrients needed to produce a big, beautiful flower within itself.

Crocus are usully forced in pebbles and water in shallow pots. Hyacinths are often forced in "bulb glasses." These are clear glass cups in hourglass shape designed to keep the bulb upright, just above the water, while the roots grow down into the water. Instead of a bulb glass, you can use a widemouthed jam jar with a nipped-in waist. Or you can plant hyacinths, paper-whites and other bulbs in flat, wide, shallow ceramic containers. They must be deep enough to hold the bulbs upright. Most five-and-dime stores and garden supply centers offer wide, shallow decorative "bulb pans" in finished ceramic for this purpose.

Also suitable for forcing are clay pots called "bulb pans" (wider than they are deep), standard planting pots and the type called "azalea pots" (which are a little deeper than bulb pans). They can be clay or plastic. The bulbs that stand tallest at flowering—tulips, for instance—do well in standard pots. Bulbs forced in soil do best in pots twice as deep as the bulb height.

Bulbs are most attractive when forced in groups of six or eight to a container. Bulbs for forcing are planted very close together: Eight or nine tulip bulbs will fit an 8-inch pot. However, you can fit as many as 20 crocus bulbs in a pot of that size.

If you are planning to chill the bulbs in an outdoor pit, then you will want to use regular planting pots rather than ornamental ceramic containers. If the bulbs are to be chilled in a basement or garage, then you can set them out in ornamental containers. Plantings in utilitarian pots can be made more attractive by wrapping the pots, once you bring them indoors, in paper matched to your room decor or in pieces of florist's sheet moss.

Where to Chill the Pots

Pre-chilled or "for forcing" bulbs, as noted above, are the kind to choose if chilling the bulbs is going to present a problem. The length of the chilling period varies, about 12 to 13 weeks for non-chilled bulbs. Tulips must have a deep chill before they can be forced, or they won't bloom. Hyacinths, daffodils, crocus and the smaller bulbs need a chilling, too.

If you have a cold cellar, garage, uninsulated attic corner or a storage spot under uninsulated eaves, these make good choices for the chilling period. As long as the temperatures are between 35 and 48 degrees, any spot will do. An old refrigerator where temperatures can be kept between these levels is suitable, too. A popular storage place is a cold frame or well-drained pit outdoors. If you make a pit, guarantee drainage by spreading 1 inch of sand or pebbles on the pit floor. If you live in a truly cold region, line the pit with polystyrene.

Though most flowering bulbs are perfect for mixing, large pots full of a single variety are used when great splashes of color are needed.

Experiment with unusual containers—you may find that they are the key to an exotic arrangement.

If both indoor cold storage and a cold frame are available choose according to your life style. The pots kept in a cellar or other indoor cold storage must be kept watered during their chilling period. If you are likely to forget them, then chill them outdoors where nature, as a rule, will water them for you.

Timing Blooms
For big bulbs planted in soil and chilled outdoors, the Department of Agriculture and the Dutch bulb growers recommend a chilling period of 12 to 13 weeks. Pre-chilled bulbs forced in pebbles and water and chilled in a garage, in my experience, seem to be ready for their indoor life after three to five weeks. But a number of variables are involved. If outdoor temperatures go to deep cold early, then to warm in a few weeks, your bulb pots may show the kind of growth that is a signal to bring the pots indoors. You cannot garden successfully by rote, any more than you can cook successfully by rote. Set your bulbs to chill, but check them often enough to keep track of their growth. See photographs on pages 52–53.

As a generalization, once tulips have been moved indoors, they will require six to eight weeks to come into bloom. Hyacinths will require about six weeks, and daffodils and paper-whites need five to ten weeks. Smaller bulbs require only a few weeks to bloom after they have started growing. If these timings seem vague, it's because the length of time necessary for the bulbs to come into bloom depends on the individual variety and on many other factors, impossible to predict. Since blooms generally last a week to 10 days, start your bulbs a week to 10 days earlier than the date you hope to have them in bloom.

Forcing Bulbs Rooted in Soil

If you are planting your bulbs in pots full of soil, begin by washing the pots to remove any crusted minerals gathered on the inside or the outside. If planting in clay pots, soak them 24 hours before planting. Otherwise the porous clay will draw the moisture from the soil.

Since keeping the bulbs supplied with moisture and holding them upright are the functions of the soil in this type of gardening, the composition of the soil mixture used is important. It must be porous, so water does not accumulate and rot the bulbs, but it must also retain moisture. The mixture recommended by the Netherlands Flower-bulb Institute is a combination of equal parts of all-purpose potting soil, ground peat moss and sand or vermiculite. You don't need fertilizer; remember, the bulbs have their own.

Before adding soil to the pots, place a piece of broken clay pot or a large uneven stone over the pot drainage hole to keep the soil from flowing out. Then, fill the pot

When planting bulbs, tips should be showing just above the pot rim.

with enough soil so bulb tips will reach about ¼ inch below the pot rim. Don't pack the soil—that makes it harder for the roots to grow. Keep it loose and fluffy. Don't press the bulbs into the soil; set the broad bases gently on it. The bulbs should be almost, but not quite, touching, as shown in the photos. When planting tulips, place the bulbs so that their flat sides press against the sides of the pot; the first big leaf of the plant will face outward and make a prettier display. When the planting is complete, sift soil over the bulbs to fill the pot to ¼ inch from the rim top. Do not pack down the soil. The tip of the bulb should be showing above its surface. Tamp the soil down gently with your fingertips.

Label Your Pots

The next step is to label the pots. Flat wooden or plastic labels are sold by garden supply centers. Recording the type of bulb, the planting date and the projected bloom date in a special plant date-book will prove useful later. Although you may think you won't forget what is planted in which pot, you will. If you add to the label the date when you expect the bulb to be ready to bring indoors, you'll be that much surer when you examine your pots during the chilling period of what should be happening and when. Place that date in your date book, with a notation a few weeks before the anticipated date. Begin examining the pot at the earlier date, just in case surprises in weather or in the bulbs themselves have thrown your predictions off.

Labels not only help identify what's what, but also build a private storehouse of information. Keep track of when you planted

each bulb and when it bloomed this year. Next year when you are wondering how long it took certain bulbs to bloom, you'll have much more exact information than any book can give you. It will be what actually happened at your house, with bulbs you have handled, in your particular growing and gardening space and climate.

Cold Treatment

If your bulbs are to be chilled in a storage pit outside, set them close together, water them well and cover them. Almost any kind of covering that lets air circulate and lets water in is suitable. You can cover the pots with loose, clean sand (not sea sand, which contains salt), with peat of any kind or with sawdust. Shredded leaves are suitable as long as they are very loosely packed. In regions where there is hard frost, professional growers use polystyrene, but it is so light that it blows away readily, and I find it messy to deal with. Bits always cling to the pots, and it seems to me I am tracking the stuff around the house for months after I bring the pots in. If you do use polystyrene, cover it with chicken wire or screening

Carefully add soil to bulbs; don't bury the bulbs or pack the soil.

Roots coming through drainage hole is a sign of well-established bulb growth; remove planting from pot and check root ball.

of some sort that will keep it from blowing all around the yard. Burlap bags, held down with bricks, make a good pit cover.

The big advantage of polystyrene is that it does not freeze. You will find you want to haul the pots from the pit during freezing weather, and if the covering material has frozen together, the pots can be impossible to get at. Since the pit pots must be watered during this chilling period—either by nature or by you—choosing a packing material that stays loose is important, especially in the very cold areas of the country.

Your next move is to wait, watering the plants every week or 10 days if it doesn't rain, until the time when the plants should be ready to bring in.

Forcing Bulbs
Rooted in Pebbles and Water
Planting bulbs in pebbles and water is a simple procedure. Once you have selected containers (deep enough to hold the bulbs comfortably), line the bottoms

with pebbles 1 to 2 inches deep. Set the bulbs, almost, but not quite, touching, in the pebbles. (Hyacinths are often rooted in bulb cups or glasses. Narcissus and smaller bulbs are often rooted in pebbles and water. Tulips are usually rooted in soil.) Fill in around the bulbs with more pebbles, leaving the top half of the bulbs free. The purpose of the pebbles is to keep the bulbs upright after tall leaves and stems grow.

Fill the pebble bowls with water so that the very bottom of the bulb bases meets the water, and keep the water at that level during the chilling period. If the bulbs are in glasses, fill the glasses level with the bulb base and keep the level there during the chilling period.

Next, move the bulbs, whether in pebbles and water, or just in water alone, in a cold dark place. Temperatures should be between 35 and 50 degrees. Cover the bulb tops with upturned pots or paper cones, to exclude all light. This will keep the leaves and stems

growing straight when growth begins.

Check Pots Periodically
One of the most important steps in forcing bulbs is to bring them indoors to light and warmth at the right moment. In about 12 to 13 weeks, the bulbs being chilled in an outdoor pit should be ready to bring in. But start checking them at 10 weeks or even earlier if the weather has been unexpectedly mild. They may be ready to bring in. Check bulbs growing in soil, pebbles and water, or just water, about 10 weeks after setting them out.

The bulbs are ready to move to light and warmth when they have developed strong roots and when stems about 3 inches tall are showing.

Some of the signs of good root growth are illustrated. Roots poking their way through the drainage hole of the pot suggest good root growth. Lift the root ball out and have a look.

When the bulbs are growing in pebbles and water, root growth filling the container is easy to spot, and if top growth is sufficient, about 3 inches, then they are ready for indoor growth.

Hyacinths are a little different. These are ready to be forced into bloom when the flower bud, which grows close to the top of the bulb, is lifted well out of the bulb neck.

Forcing the
Bulbs into Bloom
Once the bulbs are ready for forcing into flower, move them indoors or upstairs, as the case may be, to the coolest spot you have. The ideal spot is a room, a closed-in porch or a windowsill where temperatures are around 60 degrees. The flowers may blast, or wither, if they are suddenly

brought into a really warm room. Do not place them in strong sunlight at once. Rather, set them near light or in a north window or on the floor below a window. After a few weeks the stems should begin to grow strongly, to elongate and become green.

When the plants are growing well and buds have appeared (the hyacinth will already be budded when you first move it into the warmth), the plants can be moved to their permanent display spot in good light or near bright sun. The best temperature for bringing forced bulbs into flower is about 65 degrees. However, once the blooms are well underway they generally stand up to temperatures that are higher, around 70 degrees. But they don't take well to 75 and 80 degrees. And that shouldn't be surprising. These are plants whose normal blooming takes place in early or midspring, not in the high heats of summer.

Care of Forced Bulbs

Watching the bulbs unfurl their colors is a delight and takes place over a period of weeks. During this period of growth, keep the soil evenly damp but never soggy wet. When you water, water until enough has been poured on so water seeps into the pot saucers. An hour later, remove any excess water left in the saucers.

Once the blooms have opened, keep the soil dryer than during the growth period. The blooms will last longer if they aren't in moist soil. They also will last longer in cooler air. If the air temperature in your home is at 70 degrees, you can help the flowers last by airing out the rooms often, and by misting near the plants several times daily. Blasts of hot, dry air from heaters and stale, hot, dry air—the enemies of most houseplants—certainly don't help plants that

If root ball of planted bulbs lifted from pot is rootbound, it is time to to bring the pot into warmth and light for bloom.

usually grow in the cool, moist air of early spring.

The temperature requirements of the bulbs differ. Tulips and hyacinths can stand 65 to 70 degree temperatures best, while daffodils, paper-whites and crocus do best if the temperatures aren't over 65 degrees. You can help offset the effects of high heats by moving the pots to cooler locations at night. The floor, for instance, is usually cooler than table or sill height.

As existing blooms die, cut away their stems. Since you are growing several plants in each pot, removing dead flowers and browning foliage helps keep the pot pretty right to the end. When the last blossom has gone by, the show is over, but not before.

Try Forced Bulbs Outdoors

Once your indoor bulbs have bloomed, are they over and done with? Many gardeners throw the bulbs away, but I have always planted them outdoors. It doesn't take much effort, and I've often

been rewarded by a spring show of color one or two years later.

Before they can be planted outdoors, however, the foliage must be allowed to ripen and die away. Ripen means to brown, then dry, and this goes on over a period of many weeks. The number of weeks depends on the plant. Set the bulbs outdoors in a sunny spot in their pots, and keep them well watered during the ripening process. By the time the foliage has died away, the ground should have warmed enough for digging. Set the bulbs in a naturalized site. Since their next move isn't guaranteed, and they may come up peaked or not at all, don't use up precious gardening space on a home for them. A good location for most spring bulbs is under deciduous trees or shrubs, where the bulbs are somewhat shaded in summer but exposed to sun in fall and spring.

If you mark the planting spot with a label, you'll be able to see the planting in early fall. Scatter a little all-purpose fertilizer over it,

and again in early spring scratch in a little more fertilizer. The foliage may come up, but the bulbs may fail to bloom. Don't be discouraged. Deep in the ground, the bulb may be dividing itself and starting new plants on their way to bloom next year or in years to come.

Don't try to force this year's bulbs into bloom again next year. The forcing process exhausts them, and chances are they won't do a thing. Amaryllis is the exception (see page 57).

Other Bulbs

The tiny bulbs that bloom in early spring are among the most rewarding forced bulbs. When planted in small containers suited to their proportions, they make charming displays in delicate colors.

The Little Bulbs

Forced crocus are usually offered in florists' shops, and are delightful when planted in concert with other bulbs as illustrated at left. But there are many other small bulbs that have been neglected for home forcing. *Iris reticulata,* a small, exotically shaped iris which grows to about 7 inches tall, is one of the loveliest of the small bulbs to force indoors. Planted eight to ten in a 6- to 8-inch pot, the straight, slender foliage and lovely color make a show that is much admired. Outdoors they generally bloom toward the beginning of midspring, but they can be forced indoors in January or February.

Grape hyacinth *(muscari)* is another little bulb that looks wonderful group-planted in a shallow bowl. There are shades of blues

---

When planting small bulbs, don't hesitate to group them with their larger relations—they point up each other's beauty.

to mix and match with white. Smaller and more delicate than *Iris reticulata,* these bulbs grow about 5 or 6 inches tall, and produce clusters of tiny buds amid exquisitely slender, grasslike leaves. Plant grape hyacinth in bunches, in single or mixed colors. Blue on blue looks wonderful, but there's something equally delightful about blues mixed with crisp white, with bright green foliage as a background.

Scilla, in blue or white, is another small bulb that forces successfully. The delicate bell-shaped flowers make a lovely display.

Other small bulbs to try include snowdrops, which need very cool indoor conditions (since they are the earliest of spring bloomers outdoors), and glory-of-the-snow, a shade smaller but similar. Glory-of-the-snow blooms just at the beginning of midspring and forces fairly well in moist conditions. Snowflake, which is 9 to 10 inches tall, is another small bulb to try indoors.

None of these is particularly difficult to force into bloom. The reason these small bulbs are seldom seen is because the displays they make aren't showy, and the professional growers have more success selling showy displays than they have selling subtle ones. But if you know and love flowers, a potful of tiny bulbs in the right setting has almost more appeal than a great big potful of the larger bulbs.

Handling the Smaller Bulbs

Forcing the smaller bulbs into bloom differs little from handling the larger bulbs. Because of their size, they force more quickly once brought into warmer temperatures. (Be careful of those that bloom earliest, like crocus, which begin to look "poorly" when the indoor temperature is over 65

degrees.) With today's fuel shortages, more homes are maintained close to 65 degrees. And more homes have cooler rooms where individual thermostats are kept at low. However, apartments still tend to be heated to 70 degrees and often higher. For such homes, the cool-loving small bulbs described here aren't the best bet for indoor forcing.

The little bulbs are considerably less expensive in quantity than the

Proper planting depth and adequate spacing for small bulbs is shown.

Sprinkle soil in and around bulbs for support; gently firm the soil.

A *very* glorious amaryllis, with five trumpets, in bloom.

large ones, so try a half-dozen or so of each one that intrigues you. If your home conditions turn out not to suit them, the loss won't be great. If they succeed, you will be enchanted.

For smaller bulbs, select shallow containers. A bulb pan is so large in proportion to the size of the smaller bulbs that it isn't the best choice, but an 8- to 12-inch clay pot saucer is excellent. Plastic pots 3 or 4 inches across will hold four to ten of the smaller bulbs comfortably and will show them off well. The really tiny ones are delightful in a pretty cup. If bottle cutting is a hobby in your house, cut some clear glass bottles about 8 inches from the base; layer the base with small charcoal chips, then with pebbles; add a little potting soil; then plant small bulbs in a close group.

When planting the smaller bulbs don't make the common mistake of burying them too deep in the potting soil. Like the taller bulbs, they should be set on the soil at a level that brings their tips close to the container rim. However, with *Iris reticulata* I've found it best to set the soil level to bring the bulb tips a little below that recommended for taller bulbs. Having the side of the pot to lean against seems to give the slender stems a little needed support. I find they stand taller longer if planted this way.

After sifting the soil around the bulbs, firm them into the soil with your fingertips. Don't pack the soil to cement, but only enough to give the bulbs support. The larger bulbs have some support for the foliage in the size of the bulb itself, while the smaller bulbs can offer little help to the foliage. In the ground outdoors, the bulb is buried relatively deep. Set on top of soil in pots for indoor forcing,

support is scant, and the toppling of foliage spoils displays. This is one reason small bulbs are often potted up in containers such as those shown in the photographs on page 55.

Another way to handle the small bulbs is to start them in large pots. If you are going to chill them in an outdoor pit, you won't want to use your best china to begin them. Start with an 8-inch bulb pan and plant the bulbs about 1 inch apart. Remove them to the outdoors for their chilling period and bring them in when they have good roots and 1 to 2 inches of top growth. Remember, they start out in a cool room, 50 to 60 degrees. In three or four weeks, top growth of varieties such as scilla should be 6 to 8 inches high. Choose a day when the plant is ready for watering.

Layer pebbles in the container, with water just below the surface of the pebbles. This time, pack the bulbs close enough so there seems to be no spaces between them. The bulb plants will be held upright by firmed soil. Tip the pot over and work each little bulb loose from the mass of soil, keeping as much of the root ball intact as possible. Lifting as much soil as you can with each plant, transplant to display container.

After blooming is over, the small bulbs may be transplanted outdoors (see the instructions for large bulbs on page 53).

The Glorious Amaryllis
The first time I ever saw an amaryllis in bloom was years ago at a flower show in New York. The size of the trumpet-shaped blooms was a shock, but I wasn't pleased with the straight-up foliage that went along with them. Since then, I've forced amaryllis and

have discovered that their colors are truly glorious and that the foliage isn't always miles high. Sometimes it is of a size quite in proportion to the bloom. For the beginner, the amaryllis is surefire. Almost more important, it is ideal for the impatient grower because it comes into bloom so fast that you think you actually might see it growing.

Unlike other bulbs forced indoors, the amaryllis needs no chilling either before or after you buy the bulbs. Furthermore, it needs very little attention to come into bloom. I've seen great big amaryllis bloom from neglected bulbs, without soil, in a box on a windowsill. I've seen bulbs survive after blooming in an office despite the most absolute neglect, and attempt to bloom again just a few months later. The fact that an amaryllis survives neglect doesn't mean it should be ill-treated, but if you are an absent-minded gardener, this is the bulb to try indoors.

Ready-to-plant amaryllis bulbs are sold in fall and winter. (They make wonderful holiday gifts, by the way.) They will come into bloom three or four weeks after planting, and the blooms last a week or two—sometimes longer.

You can plant these beauties in a group, but I think a single bulb to a 6- or 8-inch pot makes a proportionate display. Each bulb usually produces three or more trumpet-shaped flowers, and they look a little odd unless the container is of a size that bears some relationship to the size of the blooms. Plant the bulbs in soil or in pebbles and water (see page 52). Keep them in a sunny east, west or south window. They like average house temperatures,

Plant the amaryllis in a pot that is 2 inches larger in diameter.

provided the heat doesn't go above 72 or below 55 degrees.

Bringing an Amaryllis Back into Bloom

Not only is the amaryllis certain to bloom in a few weeks, but it can be brought back into bloom if handled with a little loving care. If you are planning to bring the bulb back into bloom the next year, set it out in all-purpose potting soil. Provide 1 to 2 inches of small gravel in the base of the pot for drainage. Bring the soil level close to the tip of the bulb. After blooming, cut the flowering stem off at its base, and set the pot out of the way but in good light. Keep the soil evenly moist, not soggy, until August. Then rest the bulb in a dark corner, or preferably in a dark closet, and let it dry out for eight weeks.

After this rest period, the bulb is ready for another try at blooming. Bring it from its hideaway and re-move all the dead foliage. Work carefully—you don't want to

Add soil to within 1 inch of pot rim so bulb shows only this much.

damage the bulb. Prepare a new pot, adding 1 to 2 inches of small gravel for drainage and filling with a good all-purpose potting soil. Plant the bulb, set it in good light (a sunny east, west or south window) and resume the regular watering schedule.

At this stage, the experts suggest no feeding. Theoretically, the feeding from January to August has provided the bulb with all the nutrients it needs to produce its flower.

Just how quickly the bulb will resume growth and come into bloom depends on many factors. This is not as predictable as it was the first time around, when the bulb had been specially prepared by growers for quick blooming. However, within the next two or three months, the bulb will grow and usually will produce a new set of trumpets.

In time, amaryllis bulbs will produce offsets—babies. Separate and plant the offsets. They should bloom in about three years.

FROM PROPAGATION: AN ENDLESS SUPPLY

One of the most fascinating of all ways to add to your collection is to propagate the houseplants you and your friends already have. To the uninitiated, the best known way of increasing the number of plants on hand is to sow seeds (see pages 30–45), but the fastest (usually) and easiest way to a whole new family of plants is to divide the plant materials you have on hand.

Branch tips, stems and leaves severed from the parent plants grow root systems of their own when set in water, moist sand, vermiculite or soil, and the process is endlessly intriguing to watch. Each plant group has its own method of reproducing from plant parts. Some plants reproduce by rooting from cut leaves, and this means of propagation is called "leaf cutting." African violets and the beautifully marked fancy-leaf begonias reproduce this way.

Other plants, including a majority of plants with fibrous stems, reproduce from cut young branch tips. This is propagation by "tip" or "stem cutting." Many plants, even some of the plants that can be reproduced from leaf or tip cuttings, can also be propagated by "division"; that is, by breaking apart and replanting the root system. Plants that cannot be propagated by division are those with a single main root—geraniums, for example.

The most intriguing of all propagation methods is called "air layering"—inducing root growth on the stem. It is the method used to propagate some very tall plants that have a tendency to lose their lower leaves while the tops remain vigorous but ungainly. Dracaenas and aralias are two houseplants propagated most often by air layering.

How do you know which method to use with which plant? Following are lists of the most commonly grown houseplants, grouped according to the four propagation methods. You will also find instructions for each method. Beginning on page 73 are instructions for potting and caring for brand-new and older plants.

The first method, popular houseplants propagated by tip or stem cuttings, is the easiest and fastest way to multiply your houseplants. I recommend that you try this method first.

Tip Cuttings

For all practical purposes, propagation by tip cuttings falls into two categories—succulent-type and woody-type tip cuttings. These categories describe two very different kinds of plant stems.

Instant Plants from Tip Cuttings

Wax begonias—the begonias with shiny, cupped, reddish-green or green leaves (grown outdoors as well as indoors)—are an example of succulent-type tip cuttings. Geraniums are typical of woody-type tip cuttings. Either type can be multiplied very easily by rooting stem or tip cuttings in any number of rooting materials, from water to all-purpose potting soil. However, the woody-stemmed plants gen-erally root more slowly and must be transplanted to soil at some point in their career if they are to flourish. The weak-stemmed plants, on the other hand, seem to propagate more easily and quickly, and they also seem will-ing to live on indefinitely in water.

The fastest way to have a big, lush plant display is to cut 6- to 8-inch stems from a large, flourishing succulent-type stem plant, and bunch a dozen or more of these in a small bowl full of water and let them grow there indefinitely. Among the plants you can handle this way are the wax begonias, vining plants like wandering Jews, Swedish-ivy and vining philodendrons. (See pages 60–61 for other plants that will grow in water.) Placed in light similar to that in which the parent grew, your instant plant will soon begin to put out new growth. As roots develop, the water in the bowl will become murky. Change it occasionally, every month or two, but check the water level often—it should remain constant.

Plants growing in water are usually handled like plants growing in soil. In one area, they should be pampered: It is important that they be fed regularly. Since many of the plants that will grow this way are foliage plants, feed all-purpose plant food. The all-purpose foods are generally offered in combinations of 5-10-5 or 7-6-19 (5% nitrogen, 10% phosphates and 5% potash, or 7% nitrogen, 6% phosphate and 19% potash). The 5-10-5 composition is recommended for young plants and the other composition for older plants.

Bathrooms, because of the high humidity, are ideal homes for many foliage plants. These are easily propagated from cuttings.

Use a glass rooter, in a sunny window, to start tip cuttings.

Multiply by Tip Cuttings

Baby's tears
  Helxine
Begonia
  Begonia bradei
  B. diadema
  B. semperflorens (will grow in water)
  'Rieger begonia'
Bougainvillea
  Bougainvillea
Browallia
  Browallia
Cactus
Calamondin
  Citrus
Chinese evergreen (will grow in water)
  Aglaonema
Coffee tree
  Coffea
Coleus (will grow in water)
  Coleus
Columnea (will grow in water)
  Columnea
Copper leaf
  Acalypha
Coralberry
  Ardisia
Croton
  Codiaeum

Cuttings with this much root growth are ready for potting.

Donkey-tail
  Sedum Morganianum
Dracaena (will grow in water)
  Dracaena
Dumbcane (will grow in water)
  Dieffenbachia
Euonymus
  Euonymus
Fuchsia
  Fuchsia
Gardenia
  Gardenia
Geranium
  Pelargonium
Gloxinia
  Sinningia
Gold dust plant
  Aucuba japonica variegata
Grape-ivy
  Cissus rhombifolia
Hawaiian Ti plant
  Cordyline
Hibiscus, Chinese
  Hibiscus rosa-sinensis
Impatiens
  Impatiens
Ivy, English (will grow in water)
  Hedera helix
Ivy, German
  Senecio mikanioides
Ivy, red
  Hemigraphis colorata

Ivy tree (will grow in water)
  Fatshedera
Jade plant
  Crassula argentea
Japanese Aralia
  Fatsia japonica
Jasmine
  Jasminium
Kalanchoe
  Kalanchoe
Kangeroo vine (will grow in water)
  Cissus antarctica
Lantana
  Lantana
Lipstick vine
  Aeschynanthus
Maple, flowering
  Abutilon
Mock orange
  Pittsporum
Mosaic plant; nerve plant
  Fittonia
Moses-in-the-cradle
  Rhoeo
Myrtle
  Myrtus
Nephythytis; arrow-head vine (will grow in water)
  Syngonium
Night jessamine
  Cestrum
Norfolk Island pine
  Araucaria heterophylla (top branch only)
Oxalis (some species)
  Oxalis
Pellionia
  Pellionia
Peperomia
  Peperomia
Philodendron (will grow in water)
  Philodendron
Pilea
  Pilea
Pink polkadot plant
  Hypoestes
Pittosporum
  Pittosporum
Pleomele
  Pleomele
Podocarpus
  Podocarpus

Polyscias
  Polyscias
Pothos; devils ivy (will grow in
  water)
  Scindapsus aureus
Prayer plant (will grow in water)
  Maranta
Purple passion plant
  Gynura
Redbird cactus
  Pedilanthus
Rosary vine
  Ceropegia woodii
Rose, miniature
  Rosa
Rubber plant; fig tree
  Ficus
Schefflera (will grow in water)
  Brassaia
Selaginella
  Selaginella
Shrimp plant
  Beloperone
Sonerila
  Sonerila
Spurge; euphorbia
  Euphorbia
Star of Bethlehem
  Campanula fragilis
Succulents (also by
  leaf cutting)
Swedish ivy (will grow in water)
  Plectranthus
Tahitian bridal veil
  Gibasis
Wandering Jew (will grow
  in water)
Wax plant
  Hoya
Zebra plant
  Aphelandra

Rooting Tip Cuttings

An important thing to remember when you set out to root tip cuttings, in either the succulent or woody category, is that you must start with good plant material. Plants like wandering Jew or the wax begonia, for instance, show little variation in their stems. They are jointed from top to bottom, and leaves sprout from each node (joint); except for the new tip ends, most stems are of similar thickness. When you are planning to multiply one of these plants, almost any stem tip will do, and most will root as readily from a section cut from the middle of the stem as they will if cut from a stem tip.

When you are dealing with the majority of houseplants that root from tip cuttings, however, you are dealing with plants whose stems have a rather fibrous or woody content. The older stems are thick and really woody, especially at the base near the soil. The stem tips are usually succulent, quite soft and break very easily. The old growth roots much more slowly than new growth, and sometimes it will not root at all. The very newest growth also may fail to form a root, and it will rot more easily during the rooting process. Growth that is somewhere between old and new is best for rooting, so choose a fairly new tip end that has six or eight pairs of leaves.

Be careful to choose a branch that won't spoil the look of the parent plant. If the parent plant has become old and woody—as geraniums often do during the middle of the winter—you may want to cut it back severely. In this case, cut tip ends from each of the branches; then cut the branches close to the base, leaving just a few stubs, 2 to 3 inches long, branching out above the main stem. The parent plant may develop a new and flourishing growth that will be ready to set outdoors when warm weather comes. Meanwhile, you'll have loads of tip cuttings with which to start young plants; these new plants should be ready to bloom indoors in late spring.

When cutting tips, be sure to use a clean, sharp knife or a razor blade. Cut through a node when taking a cutting (the nodes are the places where pairs of leaves

"Woody" stem end of geranium is suitable for tip cutting. Be sure to take the cutting from a mature (not old) plant.

Slice through geranium stem at a node for a tip cutting to root.

Remove leaves from stem cutting; they will rot in rooting medium.

Geranium cuttings can be rooted easily in vermiculite or water.

sprout from the stems). Each cutting should be long enough to have two or three pairs of leaves at the top and at least 2 to 3 inches of stem below them to insert in the rooting medium.

What happens if you cut elsewhere than through a node? Nothing disastrous. However, the nodes are where plants form roots from stem cuttings. If there is a piece of stem below the node when the cutting is inserted in the water, that extra inch will generally rot, and the rot may affect the rest of the cutting. Meanwhile, the portion of the "between-nodes" stem that has remained on the parent plant will do nothing for the plant. It will wither and die, usually back to the node beneath, where new leaves or new branches will begin to grow.

After you have taken your cutting, cut away all leaves except the top two or three pairs. This leaves the bottom end clear of leaves. This is the end that goes into the rooting medium. If you let leaves

remain on this portion, they will rot and may harm the rooting stem. Unless the leaves are in the air and light, above the rooting medium, they won't help the stem so it is best to remove them.

Tip cuttings will root in any of several growing mediums. A "growing medium" is simply the general term used to describe the material plants grow in. Water is the easiest medium in which to root tip cuttings. It's easiest in that everybody has some, and also you can use it in almost any glass container. Charming little glasslike balls to hang in front windows are quite popular. The balls have openings at the top that are meant for rooting tip cuttings. They also serve as permanent containers for the types of water plants described on page 58. However, glass containers of any type will do. I have had luck with lightly colored beer bottles, but I have also rooted many plants in little ceramic vases that my daughter has brought home from pottery classes.

You can also root tip cuttings in soil or soillike material. The advantage then is that the young cuttings have root balls rather than just roots when it comes time to transplant them. However, rooting in water seems to be surer with some plants, and somewhat faster.

Other materials suitable for rooting tip cuttings include vermiculite or perlite, potting soil or clean sand. Vermiculite, perlite and sand (not sea sand, which is loaded with salt) hold the plants upright and induce something of a root ball. Vermiculite, in addition, holds water well, so that the danger of the rooting medium drying out is minimized.

Potting soil results in a better root ball, I think, but I find that more cuttings rot in potting soil than in the other mediums

The most effective arrangements are often the simple ones. Here wax begonias mixed with fancy-leaf varieties and a hint of salvia.

Dig a rooted offset to create a single new plant. If you do this carefully without disturbing the parent plant, both will thrive.

recommended. If you do use potting soil, choose a soil suited to the plant. Commercial soil mixtures include all-purpose potting soil, African-violet soil, cactus soil and terrarium soil. When I use potting soil for rooting tips, I generally add a double portion of vermiculite to keep the soil light and help it retain moisture.

If you are using a rooting medium other than water, containers may be regular plant pots (put a few pebbles in the bottom to insure good drainage), plastic refrigerator boxes or wooden or pressed peat flats of the type sold for starting seedlings.

After you have taken the cutting, let the tip dry a few minutes. (If it's a Christmas cactus, let it dry 24 hours.) Many growers have good results from dipping the base of the cutting into a commercial root-promoting hormone.

Insert the cutting to a depth of 1 to 2 inches in the soil or water. If you are planting in a solid material, firm the material around the base of the cutting. Keep the rooting medium constantly moist, except for cacti, succulents and plants noted as preferring soil on the dry side. A little tent of plastic will help retain moisture if you are going to be away for more than a day or so. Don't keep the soil soggy, or the cutting may rot. Don't let it dry out, or it may wither. Gentle warmth, between 70 and 75 degrees, helps form roots quickly.

Set the plants in light, but not for more than an hour or two of direct sun daily, until the cuttings show signs of new growth. After that, place the cuttings in the light in which the parent plant thrives.

Root Divisions

Multiplying your plants by dividing the roots of existing plants is another of the propagation methods that results instantly in lots more plants. Whenever a pot plant develops more than one main stem that grows up from the soil, it can be divided. These roots are also referred to as "offsets." Not only will dividing plant roots give you more plants, but this method is often also important to the health of existing plants. When a many-crowned plant has filled its pot to the edges and isn't flourishing, it probably needs to be divided and repotted.

Multiply by Root Division

African violet
 Saintpaulia
Alpine strawberry
 Fragaria
Anthurium
 Anthurium
Asparagus fern
 Asparagus sprengeri
Baby's tears
 Helxine
Begonia
 Begonia 'Fischer's Ricinifolia'
 B. fuscomaculata
 B. manicata 'Aureomaculata'
 B. masoniana (Iron cross)
 B. rex
 B. semperflorens
 'Rieger begonia'
Bromeliads, all varieties
 Bromeliad
Cacti
Caladium
 Caladium
Calathea
 Calathea
Cape primrose
 Streptocarpus
Cast-iron plant; aspidistra
 Aspidistra
Century plant
 Agave
Echeveria
 Echeveria
Episcia
 Episcia
Ferns, all varieties
Gloxinia
 Sinningia

Haworthia
  Haworthia
Leopard plant
  *Ligularia tussilaginea aureo-
    maculata*
Lily turf
  Liriope (blue)
  Ophiopogon (white)
Mexican foxglove
  Allophyton
Moses-in-the-cradle
  Rhoeo
Orchid, all varieties
Palm, all varieties
Peace lily
  Spathiphyllum
Peperomia
  Peperomia
Piggy-back plant
  Tolmiea
Prayer plant
  Maranta
St. Augustine grass
  Stenotaphrum
Screw pine
  Pandanus
Selaginella
  Selaginella
Silver squill
  Scilla violacea
Snake plant
  Sansevieria
Spider plant; airplane plant
  Chlorophytum comosum
Strawberry geranium
  Saxifraga-stolonifera
Sweet flag
  Acorus
Umbrella plant
  Cyperus
Unguentine plant; aloe
  Aloe vera

Methods of Root Division

There are two methods commonly used to divide plants. The easiest way is to remove a portion of the existing root from the plant right in its pot. The other is to turn out the entire root system and pull apart the roots. The first method causes the plant little disturbance and is used when you want to take just one or two divisions from a healthy plant. The second method is used when you want to start a lot of new plants, or when a plant has become crowded in its pot.

The best time to take offsets is when the parent plant is nearing peak growth. The season of peak growth varies from plant to plant. As a general rule, it occurs in spring or summer.

To remove offsets, hold the pot surface at eye level so that you can see just how the offsets are grouped. Select one or two good-looking clumps of leaves as your transplanting targets. Put the pot down and, with a sharp knife, cut down into the soil all around the clump. Then push the knife firmly into the soil, slant it under the clump and heave up gently to loosen the root ball from the parent clump. Lift the clump, with as much root ball and soil as possible, into moist vermiculite or a mixture of soil and vermiculite.

Firm the root ball into place in its new home, moisten lightly with lukewarm water and set in the light in which the parent grew but out of direct sun for awhile.

Fill the hole left by the vanished clump in the parent plant pot with soil, and the parent should continue to grow without any sign of disturbance.

Dividing the entire root system of a potted plant is a little more complex than the removal of a single offset. It is, however, a system for multiplying plants that is almost always successful, provided the baby plantlets are handled properly.

Many large plants—the spider plant, for instance—are made up of several small plants. The first step in dividing these is to turn the root system out of its pot. With low-growing plants, spread your fingers across the top of the pot, turn the pot upside down, rap the pot rim sharply on a sink edge, and the plant will usually slide into your cupped palm.

In order to have lots of young plants in a hurry, divide all the offsets of the parent plant and pot them separately.

If it resists, rap it again on the sink edge. If it continues to resist, slide a sharp knife all around the inside of the plant pot, rap it on the sink once more and it will slip out.

If taller plants are in pots so large that your hand won't span their tops, slide a knife along the inside edge of the pot, tap the outer top of the pot all around on the sink edge. Then spread a big blanket of newspapers on the floor, and slide the plant out onto it, sideways.

Once the plant is out of its pot, shake away any loose soil to expose the root ball. If the plant has become pot bound, the soil will be so tightly twined around with roots that you probably won't find any loose dirt at all (see page 74).

The next step, working very gently with your fingers and a pencil or a dullish knife, is to force the roots of each clump of the plant free from the root ball. Once the twining outer roots have been loosened, you will begin to see how the separate smaller root clumps have grown together to form a big plant. Grasp the leaves or stems of the outer plant clumps and tug these loose from the main root ball. When the outer clumps have been freed, loosen the inner clumps. As you work, preserve as much root as possible. If you find a root you can't get free, cut it. A clean cut is healthier for the plant than a messy break.

Now it is time to pot the baby plants. Choose soil (see page 76) in which the parent grew and lighten it a little with a handful of vermiculite. Place the soil and pot in lukewarm water so the soil will

An African-violet collection is a real collector's item. Give it a special setting, and keep a supply of cuttings ready for replacements.

draw moisture from the base; when the soil is moist, plant the babies (see page 73).

How many babies to each new pot depends on what you plan to do with the plants. You can turn one big plant into two smaller plants or into dozens of small plants. Even a small spider plant will be composed of as many as six or eight offsets. A single baby plant in a huge pot looks forlorn, so unless you really want dozens of new plants in a hurry, plan to pot several of the offsets together in each new pot.

Care of Newly Potted Divisions

The newly planted divisions require the same care as the parent plant. When they have just been repotted, keep them back a little from the light and don't allow them any direct sunlight for several days. Direct sun draws moisture from the leaves. While the roots of these babies are struggling to reestablish their ability to draw water and nourishment from the soil, they aren't of as much help as usual in maintaining leaf moisture. This means that the babies can wither severely in just a few hours of direct sun.

Some growers, especially when propagating dozens of young offsets, tent the pots with thin plastic to help keep moisture around the struggling babies. Another way to maintain a moist atmosphere is to mist the area in which they are growing several times a day.

Yet another way, especially suitable in the dry heat of winter, is to place the pots on a tray of pebbles (keep the water level below, not touching, the pot level). You can also place a bowl of water nearby so that some moisture is constantly being drawn into the atmosphere. Fresh circulating air

helps to keep the new plants healthy.

Water the young plants often enough to keep them evenly moist. Those plants that prefer to be kept on the dry side—succulents, for instance—should be watered less often.

Leaf Cuttings

The way that the African violet reproduces from leaf cuttings is typical of the reproduction system of many plants. As you will see on page 70, there are other ways that leaves produce roots, but the way that African violets do it is the most common.

Multiply by Rooting Leaves

African violet
 Saintpaulia
Begonia
 Begonia 'Fischer's Ricinifolia'
 B. fuscomaculata
 B. manicata 'Aureomaculata'
 (Leopard begonia)
 B. masoniana (Iron cross)
 B. rex
Cape primrose
 Streptocarpus
Donkey-tail
 Sedum morganianum
Gloxinia
 Sinningia
Hens-and-chickens
 Echeveria
Jade plant
 Crassula argentea
Kalanchoe
 Kalanchoe
Peperomia
 Peperomia
Wax plant
 Hoya

Rooting Leaf Cuttings from African Violets

African violets are so easy to propagate by leaf cuttings that

Develop new plants from African-violet leaf cutting by rooting cuttings individually or in groups in African-violet soil, vermiculite, a combination of African-violet soil and vermiculite, or water.

you can make many plants from a single parent. The blooms of African violets literally come in dozens of lovely different colors and markings. Once you have successfully rooted a few leaves of your own, you can beg and borrow single leaves from the various types you come across and create a glorious collection without investing a penny.

First step is the choice of a good leaf. Select a leaf that is strong, healthy and fairly mature. Using a clean, sharp knife, slice the stem from the parent plant about 2 inches from the leaf's bottom edges. I usually take two or three cuttings for every baby plant I hope to have, because I have found that some of the rooting leaves fail. Choose your leaves from places on the parent plant where many leaves seem to be close together (you don't want to spoil the appearance of the parent).

Have ready a glass of lukewarm water or one of the leaf-rooting setups illustrated here: a plastic bag one-quarter filled with moist vermiculite; a small plastic pot filled with African-violet soil or vermiculite; a large plastic box— a discarded refrigerator box, for instance—filled with either African-violet soil mixed half and half with vermiculite or vermiculite only.

One of the most common ways to root African violets is in a glass of water. Foil is secured over and around the glass, and the leaves are inserted in thin slots in the foil, holding the leaves upright (see illustration above). The plastic bag approach is used when there is a shortage of window shelf space on which to stand rooting leaves. Tied loosely, the plastic bag can be thumb-tacked to the window jamb until leaves have formed. The procedure to follow when you want to root lots of leaves is to group them together in a container, such as an old refrigerator box.

You can also root one or two leaves of each of several varieties in African-violet soil and vermiculite in a large old washbowl or some other pretty, wide, shallow container. Once rooted, the plants needn't be transplanted; and when they come into bloom, just a few months later, the bowl makes a truly beautiful display.

Water, vermiculite and African-violet soil (alone or mixed with vermiculite) are all suitable for propagating leaf cuttings. The choice of a rooting medium is a matter of convenience. Water rooting seems to result in fast root growth; however, you may lose some of the babies when you transplant them to soil. Some just seem to fail. Those that succeed will need time to take hold. Cuttings rooted in soil transplant more successfully and suffer little check in growth. But, in truth, you will find that however you root your cuttings, most of them will succeed and transplant without much trouble.

Where do you place the cuttings to root? I recommended a sunny window, but that is subject to many definitions, as many as the recipes for success with African violets. In my own experience, African violets adapt to many kinds of light. In moderate and hot climates, they succeed in bright north windows. In cool regions, they may do better in east and west windows, where there is some direct sun daily. In Connecticut, I grew them in a south picture window, a few feet back from the big panes, in light that was filtered by slightly taller plants. That window was covered by an awning in the summer, so the plants never received the direct rays of the summer sun.

African violet babies seem most successful when set in the same kind of light in which the parents grew. It's a good idea to set the cuttings to root where the parent lives for another reason: African violets tend to sulk, sometimes for months, after they have been moved, and this applies to the root cuttings, too. Until the leaves begin to root, set the leaves back somewhat from the window.

How long will the leaves take to root? It's hard to say. Some take months, others just weeks. It's

easy to tell when the plant has rooted when it is growing in water —the roots are visible. When growing in a plastic bag filled with vermiculite, you will see fine threads of roots meshing around the bits of vermiculite. The real sign that the plant is ready to transplant is when several sturdy baby leaves begin to grow from the parent stem. They are incredibly tiny at first, but soon begin to assume the shape of the parent leaf and get to be 1 to 2 inches long. The longer you wait to transplant the babies, the stronger they will be—within reason. Sometimes the parent leaf withers, and that's a sign that it is time to transplant. At other times, the parent leaf stays strong. As long as it is healthy, do not separate the parent leaf from the planting. Plant the baby—roots, parent leaf and all—in the new growing medium.

What soil to plant it in? With African violets, the answer is easy: African-violet soil, either a commercial African-violet mix or your own composition of any good garden loam plus a double quantity of ground peat moss. Since commercial all-purpose potting soil already includes about one-third

peat moss, simply add an additional third of peat moss to bring the proportion up to two-thirds.

Care of African Violets

The idiosyncrasies of African violets in regard to light are noted. In my experience, they seem to bloom best when they have a few hours of direct sun daily. They also thrive under fluorescent lights.

Temperature has an effect on African violets. Flowering is less when the plants are in a hot, dry atmosphere. Temperatures between 70 and 75 degrees are fine; below 60 degrees, the plants suffer. In winter, to keep the air moist, group the plants on beds of pebbles. Keep water in the pebbles, but be sure the water level remains below the level of the pot bottoms.

African violets very often begin to flower when the plants are still quite young. Once they start blooming, they tend to keep right on blooming if the conditions described above are met.

Sometimes the pots fill with several crowns, or main plant stems. Crowded in this fashion, the violets may slow down or stop

Use a sharp knife to take leaf cutting; 2 inches of stem is enough.

Several leaves are rooted at the same time. Foil holds them in place.

blooming entirely. Separate the crowns with a clean, sharp knife. Set in African-violet soil mixed half and half with vermiculite. Propagating African violets by division this way is tricky—they don't always take.

Offsets (very small plants) sometimes form on the sides of main African-violet stems. These should be rubbed off with a pencil eraser when they are still small enough to respond to such treatment. If they become too large, the offsets may stop the plant from blooming and, in any case, will spoil its symmetry.

Water African violets often enough to keep the soil evenly moist but not soaked. Use only lukewarm water. Showers of icy water can inhibit bloom in African violets and usually cause unsightly spots on the leaves. An hour after watering, pour off any excess water in the pot saucer, so the pots won't sit in a puddle.

Rooting Leaf Cuttings from Begonias

Begonias of the types known as rhizomatous (grown from rhizomes) and those called "fancy-leaf" multiply most easily from leaf cuttings, but these leaf cuttings are handled quite differently from African-violet leaf cuttings. These begonias often can be rooted as African-violet leaves are rooted, but there's a better way.

Begin as you would for propagating African violets. Choose a healthy, sturdy leaf and cut the stem 1 to 2 inches below the leaf bottom. The leaf is then gashed and pegged to moist soil. The young plants will grow from these gashes, as shown in the illustration here.

The soil best suited for rooting begonia leaves is terrarium soil, which you'll find offered in commercial mixtures. Regular potting soil to which you have added half as much ground peat moss will do as well, and so will a similar mixture of regular potting soil and vermiculite. The important thing is to have a soil composition that stays loose and moist easily. Place the soil in a small pot on top of a layer of pebbles. It must stay moist but never soggy.

The way in which the leaf is gashed is important. Turn the leaf over, face side down (the face side is the most colorful side). Now, with the corner of a razor or with the tip of a very sharp knife, gash the major veins, as shown in the illustration. The gashes should be fairly small but must cut through the vein. Now, turn the leaf over, face side up, and lay it on the soil. Gently press it down, so it is in contact with the soil in as many areas as possible. Peg it into place with an old-fashioned hairpin, or else place one or two small pebbles on it.

Place the leaf in the same light as that in which the parent plant is growing, and keep it evenly moist but not soaked. Water the soil by filling the pot's saucer with lukewarm water any time the surface soil shows signs of drying out. If you mist the plant often, even daily, this will help to encourage growth. In a few weeks, tiny plants should develop in each or most of the cuts. Allow the leaf babies to grow until they have reached 1 to 2 inches in size before you prepare to transplant them.

The next step is most important. Tiny begonia plantlets, like the new African violets, need portions of their parent leaf top as long as it stays healthy. Before you dig up the babies, plan how to cut up the parent leaf in such a way that each baby gets the largest possible portion of parent leaf assigned to it. With a razor, and while the leaf is still pegged to the soil, cut up the leaf in the portions planned. Then, with a small trowel or pointed spoon, gently dig down under each baby and lift it up, raising as much soil clump as possible with the roots. Lift the plantlet onto a

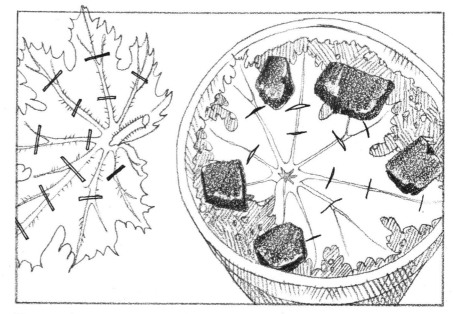

To root a begonia leaf, first gash the back of leaf; then place the leaf, cut-side down, on soil; then secure with stones.

fluffy, moist bed of African-violet soil. Set the pot that holds it into a container of lukewarm water, and you won't need to water the baby for a few days. For the first few days place the plantlets in slightly less light than that in which the parent plant grows.

Care of Begonias

Once your new leaf begonias are thriving, you'll find them easy to care for. The rhizomatous begonias have fleshy, thick stems that grow along the top of the soil with long roots below the surface. Some varieties grow upright, and others tend to cascade over pot sides. The latter are good hanging basket subjects.

Either type grows well in standard plastic or clay pots. Mature plants will succeed in all-purpose potting soil with an added portion of vermiculite or ground peat moss, African-violet soil or terrarium soil.

The best light for the begonias is a few hours of direct sun in an east or west window. Some adapt very comfortably to the light of a bright north window, especially in moderate to warm climate zones. If the stems grow long and leggy, seeming to reach for the light, and the color in your plants pales, they are telling you they need more light. If the window light is not bright, a few additional hours of light from a lamp will help.

Ideal temperatures for rhizomatous begonias are somewhere between 70 and 80 degrees. Other types of begonias seem to do well enough in cooler temperatures, but the rhizomatous types sulk in cooler air. Continuous dry heat, however, doesn't suit them either. Leaf edges tend to brown. Misting in the area of the plants helps keep the air fresher and more humid. If you can air the room out often by opening doors or windows, that will help keep them in optimum condition.

Mature begonias require evenly moist soil. If the soil dries out, leaf edges will brown. If the soil is too moist, the rhizome will rot and the plant will die. I usually bottom water begonias of this type to make sure I am not drenching the rhizome and leaving pockets of stale water to sour in its gnarly folds. If water remains in the plant saucers after an hour or so, the soil may become soggy, and that will be bad for the plants.

Because these begonias are grown for foliage and for bloom, alternate plant food types during the year. In spring and summer the plants will bloom, so in the months that precede that period—late fall and winter—feed begonias plant food for blooming plants. In late summer and early fall, feed the plants with a food intended to promote foliage growth. For frequency of feeding, follow the plant food container directions.

To keep my begonias looking wonderful, I must repot them not only when they begin to crowd their pots, but every year or two as well. Otherwise the stems begin to wither, and the whole plant may die.

From time to time when you are watering your plants, remove leaves whose edges have withered or whose stems are unattractive or have withered portions. This little grooming effort will keep the plant producing handsome foliage and will help to keep it in good health.

Occasionally, one of my begonias just ups and dies. I suspect that overwatered soil and wet rhizomes are the cause. Because it can happen, having a constant supply of new plants is a good idea.

Angel wing begonias look best when they are staked. Slender, but rigid, bramble branches can be used, or buy inexpensive cane stakes. Insert the stakes close to the plant, and use twist ties or soft wool to affix the branches to the stakes.

When new sprouts have formed and are ready for potting, cut them apart and take as much of the parent leaf as possible with each baby.

Air Layering

Air layering is the most fascinating way of all to provide yourself with new plants. However, it is a method that applies to only a few indoor plants. Air layering is a technique in which the main plant stem is wounded, then handled in such a way that the wound produces roots that then can be planted.

The type of plants multiplied by air layering are tall plants of kinds that tend to lose lower leaves. Some of our hardiest plants are included in this category; for instance, corn plant and rubber plant.

Both of these plants grow to be very tall in indoor culture. However, after they near ceiling height they seem to lose their lower leaves and all the grace and charm they had as younger plants. With luck, you can trade in such an ungainly duckling for two young charmers simply by air layering.

Multiply by Air Layering

Dracaena
   Dracaena
Dumbcane
   Dieffenbachia
Hawaiian Ti plant
   Cordyline
Japanese aralia
   Fatsia japonica
Philodendron
   Philodendron
Rubber plant
   Ficus elastica

New Growth by Air Layering

To begin air layering, select a spot between two nodes a few inches below the last pair of leaves on the plant, or at a spot where the leaves begin to thin out and become sparse. With a sharp knife,

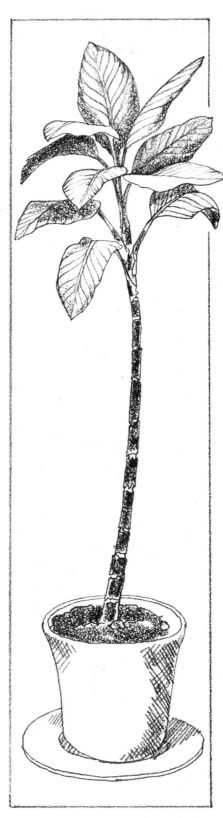

Propagate varieties like the rubber plant by air layering.

cut a slanted gash upward and almost halfway through the plant stem. Insert a clean toothpick, or the bottom end of a matchstick, into the wound to keep it propped open.

Next, thoroughly moisten a big handful of unmilled sphagnum moss. The moss should be a big wadded ball, several inches thick, and should extend 3 to 4 inches beyond the wound. Now, wrap plastic film around the ball and tie it at either end, firecracker fashion, as illustrated. You may use twist ties or string. (Twist ties are really more convenient, because you may find you need to undo the wrapping more than once.)

Within a few hours of sealing the wrapping, the inside of the plastic should film over with moisture. Check the plastic daily to make sure the moisture remains fairly constant. The roots will form only if the moss stays moist. If the plastic shows clear and dry on the inside, loosen one of the twist ties and spray the moss thoroughly, then tie the package up again securely.

Mist the plant itself often in the weeks that follow to encourage growth. Feed it well, following a regular schedule. Roots will grow quickly if the plant is kept healthy and happy, and if the moss is kept moist.

How long it will take the roots to grow will depend primarily on the plant. Some form roots in weeks, others take months. If you are air layering the plant during its peak growing season (usually spring), then roots will form more quickly.

How do you know when the roots have formed? They will show along the inner side of the plastic wrapping. Once roots have filled the moss sufficiently to show in the wrapping as healthy, solid growth, it is time to plant. Undo the plastic and check the moss to make sure there is indeed a solid root growth inside it. Then, with a clean, sharp knife, cut off the top of the plant, with its new roots, just below the bundle of moss. Handle the moss gently to avoid breaking or damaging any of the new roots.

Plant your new baby in the same kind of soil in which the parent plant grew, mixed with a portion of peat moss or vermiculite. Keep it in a slightly shaded location for a few days, misting often. When you are sure the top leaves show no sign of wilting, place the plant in the light in which the parent plant grew. Feed all-purpose plant food regularly for several months, then switch to all-purpose 7-6-19 plant food. Feed according to the container directions.

The parent plant may or may not develop new growth. It is most likely to develop new growth if some leaves are left on the bottom portion to see it through until new growth can come from the base. Feed it well and mist often, for several months. Even if new growth doesn't appear at once, it may develop later.

Potting

Potting up baby plants is one of the joys of indoor gardening. For gardeners who have propagated their own houseplants, it's a particularly happy moment. You've successfully started the plants you want, and now you are about to launch them on a real career as houseplants.

Potting New Plants

As a rule of thumb, baby seedlings are ready to pot up in their first permanent homes when they show signs of vigorous growth. That usually means when they are putting forth new leaves at a rapid rate.

There are other signs that it is time to pot. When you have several baby plants developing together in the same flat, pot or bowl, and they begin to crowd each other, it is time to pot up the largest. This will leave room for the smaller plants to develop comfortably.

Plants rooting in water are ready to pot when new growth appears on the tip ends of the cuttings. But even if little new growth is showing, as long as the cut end of the

stems have a thick growth of young roots, you may begin the potting procedure. Try one of the cuttings first, and if it succeeds, pot those that have remained in the rooting water. If the first transplant survives a week or two, chances are it's okay.

These are general rules of thumb; but where *specific* instructions have been given for certain plants, be sure to follow those procedures.

Handling Baby Seedlings

Gardeners instinctively handle very tiny plants with care when digging them up and placing them in potting material. However, there is a mistake that many beginners make when handling baby plants. When the small plant has been inserted in its little planting hole in the potting soil, it must be firmed into place, as described on the following pages. But the firming must be done in such a way that the soil around the roots isn't compacted into stiff mud.

It is vital to the growth of all plants, and in particular to the growth of young plants, that the soil in which they are growing be loose and fluffy. When putting

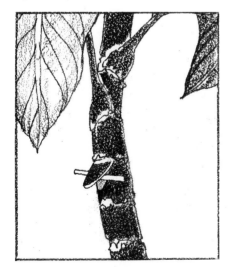
Wound stem at node point.

Wrap with moss and plastic.

Cut rooted plant from parent.

soil into the container for the new plant, whatever kind the potting mixture may be, spoon it in lightly —don't pack it in. When firming the young roots into their potting holes, do it very gently. Don't drench the plant from the top with a bucket of water. Instead, water the planting soil from the bottom by placing it in another container holding lukewarm water. You can also water the soil in the pot before you firm in the plant, and then water any added topsoil lightly with a fine spray. Drenching soil with a lot of water tends to compact it.

Repotting Older Plants

Potting new plants and repotting older plants are almost identical processes. Why and when to repot older plants? There are a number of signs that tell the gardener that older plants need repotting.

A slowdown of growth is one sign already described. When plants that have lots of room in their pots, and that are well fed, watered, lighted and loved, don't flourish, it may be because the soil in the pots has become compacted and too acidic. Fresh soil is light and fluffy and has important nutrients in it. Also, it contains little of the acids that build up from constant application of fertilizers. Older soils are the reverse, so experienced gardeners usually turn to repotting as their first effort to revitalize languishing plants.

Another sign that a healthy plant needs repotting is when it becomes crowded in its pot—"pot bound" is the word usually used. If a plant composed of many groups of stems—the spider plant, for instance—has stems growing right to the very edge of the pot, chances are it needs repotting. When a plant has a single stem— such as geraniums—how do you tell if it needs repotting? Rap the

pot edge on the sink, spread your fingers over the top of the pot and turn the plant out of its pot. If there are roots winding around and around the soil and lots of roots twining around each other at the bottom of the root ball, it is pot bound, and repotting is in order.

New Growth in Repotted Plants

The length of time it will take a newly potted or freshly repotted plant to establish itself in new soil depends on the rate of growth of the plant in question and on the care you give it. Rapid growers, like philodendrons, reestablish themselves very quickly. Slow growers, like Norfolk pines, will take a lot longer. Follow the instructions here to hasten the acclimatizing process. Once the plant takes hold, you'll see a burst of growth that's really fun to watch.

Some of the newer commercial pots have drainage holes on the insides of the bottom edges. Older types have either one large hole or several smaller holes in the pot bottoms. Generally, the large hole is so large that it will let potting soil pour through, so gardeners put a big pebble over the hole on the inside to hold in the soil. This is called "crocking." Pots with a few smaller holes may or may not need crocking. I always do it, but when soil has a lot of peat moss in it and is fibrous, it generally won't spill out of the drainage holes.

In very small pots, there is little room for a layer of drainage pebbles, and you generally don't need the drainage layer in these pots. I do add a layer, however thin, of pebbles to any pot big enough to take it (anything over 3 inches), because it improves the air circulation through the soil.

What Size Pot?

A tiny plant in a big pot looks very lost. More important is the fact that it will start out by putting all its energy into growing roots. So, choose 2- or 3-inch pots for new plantings. When repotting older plants, choose pots just one size larger than the old pots.

Pot size usually describes the horizontal measurement across the top of the pot, not vertical height. In standard pot shapes, the height of the pot is a little more than the width across the top. In the types of pots called "bulb pans" (see page 48), width and height of the pot are about the same, or the width may be more than the height.

When plants grow to the size of shrubs or trees (avocados, for instance), they should be in pots 16 to 18 inches across at the top. These big plants need repotting only every few years. Instead, every year the top few inches of soil should be replaced. The process is called "top dressing."

What Type Container?

There are several types of containers sold commercially, and these will do for most plants. For plants that prefer to be on the dry side, the best container is clay, because clay lets excess moisture evaporate. The best container material for plants that must be kept evenly moist is plastic. Plastic lets little or no moisture escape except from the surface of the soil.

What about "found containers"? Bowls, glasses, cups and pottery can be used successfully to grow many plants as long as drainage is provided.

Don't hide your work area; keep it attractive and interesting. Remember, your nursery needs all the attention you can give it.

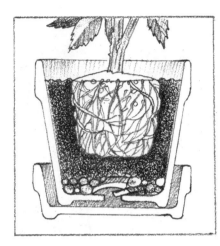

Cross section of repotting shows position of root ball and crown.

The commercial pots all have openings of one sort or another in their bottoms. Excess water flows through these openings into the saucer holding the pot. If this excess is drained off an hour or so after watering, there is little danger that the plants will be overly wet. Overwatering kills more plants than does underwatering.

In containers that have no drainage holes, you can add drainage by placing a layer of small pebbles 1 to 2 inches deep in the bottom of the container. Excess water will flow down into the pebbles and will keep the soil drained.

When planting in a large container without drainage, it is a good idea to lay 1 to 2 inches of charcoal chips (sold commercially) over the bed of drainage pebbles. The charcoal keeps the water at the bottom of the container from going sour and provides extra drainage.

Air Circulation
Inside the Container
Air circulation for the growing part of the plant is important, too, though not often discussed.

Plant roots need air as well as water and nutrients in order to flourish. This is one reason soil should be kept light and fluffy to permit the soil to retain air. Adding drainage to containers helps keep some air continually flowing from top to bottom of the plant soil. The cross section of a newly potted plant here shows the proportions of drainage materials to soil.

If you are going to use a decorative second container (cache pot), make sure this container is large enough to permit proper air circulation between it and the plant pot. Drainage pebbles and a big roomy cache pot are two things plants respond to with healthier growth.

What Kind of Soil?
There are four basic soil types sold commercially, any one of which you can approximate if you have garden soil.

All-purpose soil is recommended for most foliage plants and many flowering plants. Cactus soil is meant for plants that require exceptionally good drainage. It contains a high percentage of sand and drainage materials such as perlite. African-violet soil is also called "blooming plant soil" and has been composed to meet the needs of plants that flower. It contains enough humus to maintain an even level of moisture and is somewhat acid. It is the soil to use for plants said to need acid soil. Terrarium soil is also the type suited for bottle gardens. It contains less earth than the all-purpose soil does and lots of water-holding materials, such as humus and vermiculite.

You can make your own all-purpose potting soil by combining one part garden loam to one part humus (such as ground peat moss) and one part sand. These materials are sold by most garden

Drainage layers are provided if container has no drainage holes.

supply centers. You can also make your own African-violet and other soil mixtures. For African violets and other blooming plants, mix one part garden loam, one part sand, or vermiculite, and one part acid-ground peat moss. To make a terrarium mixture, combine sand or perlite, vermiculite, sphagnum moss and charcoal chips in equal parts. To make a cactus mixture, combine one part garden loam, one part peat moss and two parts sand or perlite.

Garden loam often contains harmful organisms, and many indoor gardeners sterilize such soil before using it for indoor plants. The best way is to start with bagged commercial products that are already pasteurized. You can buy all the ingredients described here. All-purpose potting soil is used as the basic soil for each mixture.

However, garden loam is usually good for indoor plants, and I've rarely had trouble with mine, even when I didn't pasteurize it. If you feel you should pasteurize, prepare 4 quarts of soil and heat the oven to 180°F. Place the soil in a big bowl and place the bowl inside a bigger kettle. Add 1 cup of water to the kettle and bake for

15 minutes. Turn the soil out onto clean newspaper and air it 24 hours before using.

The process of potting a baby plant or an adult plant is easy to grasp if you will look back at the cross section of a potted plant on page 76. The proportions of pot to plant size and drainage materials to soil show clearly.

Fill the pot with enough soil so that the crown (the place where stem meets the roots) of the plant will be ½ to 2 inches below the top of the pot rim. This extra space—½ inch on tiny pots, 1 to 2 inches on larger pots—makes watering easy. If you fill the pot to the very rim with soil, the water you pour onto the plant will promptly shed off, allowing little to seep down into the soil.

Rest the roots of the plant on the soil surface in the center of the pot, then pour soil in around the plant to the level of the crown. Bottom water the plant by placing it in a large container of lukewarm water or top water very gently with a fine spray.

Let the plant drain in the sink for an hour or so. Place the newly potted plant in a light source similar to that in which the parent plant grew. Be sure to keep the plant back from the light source so that it receives only a little direct sun for the first few days. After this rest period—three days is a good average—if the plant shows no signs of wilting, place it in its home spot in your collection.

After the plant has been watered a few times, you may find that the soil inside the pot has compacted a little and fallen below the crown. If so, add a bit of soil.

Mist your new plants often— daily in the beginning. It helps them to survive while the roots are establishing themselves.

Keep Your Houseplants Flourishing

Proper light is one of the most urgent needs of houseplants. Most of the popular plants will succeed in east or west windows with a few hours of sun daily. South windows in winter make great plant homes, and north windows in summer are suited to many plants. In summer, screen indoor plants in a south window from the burning sun of midday with an awning or curtains, or move the plants several feet back from the window.

Since proper light is essential to the success of your houseplants (and these requirements can differ drastically), always ask for every plant's proper horticultural name. With it, you can look up the light requirements in a reference book.

Temperatures affect houseplants, too. Most of the plants commonly sold will survive winters indoors in temperatures between 70 and 75 degrees. There are a few that prefer to be cooler. For these, frequent misting and occasional airing out of the room will help if your home is hot, or place the plants close to a cold window.

Moisture—either the lack or an overabundance of it—kills more houseplants, especially babies, than anything else. Most plants prefer to be kept evenly moist and like daily or weekly mistings, especially in winter. Some need to dry out slightly between waterings—geraniums, for example. And, of course, cacti and succulents are allowed to become quite dry on the surface. A few like to be really wet, but the piggyback plant is the only one that comes to mind. Plants billed as terrarium plants like a lot of moisture, and these should be grown in bottle gardens, terrariums or on beds of pebbles that are kept moist. (Pot bottoms must not rest in water, so keep water level below pot bottoms.) And—a final rule for the health, welfare and happiness of houseplants—put your finger in the pot before you water. It will tell you whether the soil is moist, dry or still soaking from the last watering.

INDEX

Page references appearing in **boldface** *type indicate an illustration or a photograph. Names of houseplants you can easily propagate are listed on the following pages: 30, 32, 60–61, 64–65, 67, 72.*